No Story
No Business

Special thanks to:

Richard Ollins and Locke McKenzie

What is this, anyway?

Should I list all the reasons why you should read this book, take it to heart, and implement its principles in your own life? To do so would be to commit the same mistake our hero in this book repeatedly made – the mistake that caused him to fail. The downtrend in his sales continued until one day he tried a different approach. He focused on entrancing his customers, rather than peppering them with rapid-fire facts and figures. His product was unique and clearly superior to competing brands, but that was still not enough to convince his customers to buy it. He attended sales seminar upon sales seminar, growing increasingly frustrated that his numbers were not improving. Eventually, he ran into the StorySculptor and learned to captivate customers with stories, not facts.

After that he normally didn't even make it to the end of his story before customers were practically begging to sign on the dotted line. The stories worked, not the facts. The stories created an emotional connection for the customer that pure facts simply could not, and almost all of his sales pitches were successful. He also received a flood of word-of-mouth advertising, which increased his sales even more.

This book will teach you how to achieve this level of success. Relax and enjoy reading the story of someone who set out to become a super successful salesperson and found a fun, effective way to meet his goals.

Joachim Guenster

This book will excite and inspire you, and will help you immediately improve your communication with your customers, colleagues, friends and family. You will be more persuasive, more convincing and better able to hold your audience's attention.

In other words: You will sell more, more often and you will reach your goals faster.

Who should read this book?

Whenever you want to achieve something, you need to communicate with other people. Learn to use the knowledge and techniques in this book to inspire your customers, your prospects, your boss and your partners – even your spouse.

Learn to communicate in the language our brain internalizes to sell your ideas, your wishes, and your products! In short, this book is for everyone who wants to improve his or her communication skills. Learn the basic rules and techniques that you can use to get the results you desire.

Further Information

find the latest and greatest information about selling better achieving more, negotiating more successfully at this resources

My blog: StorySculptor.net
Facebook: StorySculptorJG
Twitter: @StorySculptor
www.slideshare.net/storysculptor

1 How it all began

He was not a born salesman. Who is? Nothing about him indicated that he would one day become one of the nation's top sellers and generate astounding revenue. His childhood was inauspicious, carefree, and happy – at least until Miss Mayer, his third grade math teacher, began to overwhelm him with facts and figures. It was no fun! To make matters worse, many of his other teachers were also strict and demanded that students "buckle down" and memorize vast quantities of dry information. Our hero wasn't used to this, and he didn't like it one bit. He much preferred to spend time with his friends, inventing fantastic tales full of monsters, fairies and magic. Of course, the adults said that those mythical creatures weren't real, but our hero and his friends knew better. They were real and could be seen through the lens of their imagination. The bedtime stories were his favorite. He loved snuggling under the covers and listening to his mother describe the most incredible stories as he drifted off to sleep. Sometimes he even dreamt about them.

School seemed to get drearier every week. Our hero had lots of friends and got along well with his teachers, but he hated spending hours memorizing information that didn't captivate his attention or stimulate his mind. Gone were the fairies with their colorful, diaphanous wings; in their stead were algebra, Latin, chemistry and physics. Fortunately, school wasn't always complete torture. He enjoyed biology, for example, and became enthralled with the human brain. Certain aspects of physics, such as electromagnetic oscillations, also interested him. In biology, he learned about the human brain and in physics of electromagnetic fields. These things were easy to learn because they naturally held his attention. Many of his classmates did not fare so well and seemed to struggle in every subject. With the passage of time, our hero honed his memorization skills and developed the ability to store huge masses of facts and regurgitate them in exams. His teachers called this "learning."

When he was a university student, he began building computers and selling them to his fellow students. It all began when he salvaged a Commodore VIC 20 and sold it for a handsome profit. Soon, all his classmates wanted one, and the computers sold like hotcakes. In almost no time our hero shelved the VIC 20 and started building Commodore 64s instead. These computers were more powerful and easier to use. However, they were also more expensive, and he eventually lost a large sum of money due to the price wars of the early computer industry. Despite this financial setback, he stayed in sales and enjoyed a lucrative career by the time he had turned 30. He had an incredible memory for detail and could remember information that other salesmen never could. Additionally, he had a knack for finding and exposing flaws in competing products. He went in to every sales meeting armed with data about his product's benefits, costs, environmental impact, and market niche. He also had the same information for all competing products. Within seconds, he had most customers in the palm of his hand.

On the outside he was a seasoned professional. Inside, however, he felt burned out, frustrated, and increasingly angry. As time passed, more and more of his customers began placing orders for competing products, but he could only imagine vague reasons for them doing so. One customer admitted that he could not justify the switch, and that our hero's product was clearly superior, but stated that the superior product didn't "speak" to him anymore.

This began to happen with increasing frequency. Our hero felt sad, dejected, and disappointed in himself. He wondered if he had passed the peak of his creativity and felt like an old wolf no longer able to keep up with younger and faster members of the pack. This was not a tenable situation, and he seriously considered changing careers. *Perhaps I could become a truck driver*, he thought to himself. Dreaming of the free life on the open road. Riding into the sunset. Crazy stuff.

One day, while our hero was brooding over his disappointing sales figures, his colleague Carl noticed his melancholy. "What's wrong?" he asked. Our hero sighed in resignation. "Nothing," he whispered. Carl was the company dispatcher

and had been irritable all week due to delays in receiving new inventory. However, on this day he wore a broad smile.
"The new products have arrived and are ready for delivery," he announced, still beaming. Our hero tried to return the smile, but felt a knot in the pit of his stomach. With plenty of fresh inventory, a lack of sales would rest squarely on his shoulders.
Evidently expecting a more positive response, Carl faltered. "Have you seen a ghost or something? " He fidgeted uncomfortably. "I mean, don't you think that's great news about the inventory?"
"Yes ," sighed our hero , "but I'm losing one customer after another. "
Now the cat was out of the bag.
"Hmmmm," said the dispatcher, "maybe it 's time to talk to the StorySculptor."
The StorySculptor! How could he have forgotten that?!

Our hero leapt to his feet and practically kissed Carl.

"What a great idea!" The world suddenly seemed like a better and more hopeful place. He rushed out of the building into the parking lot, hopped in his car, and flew out of the driveway, tires screeching. Carl watched him go and thought, "Wow, what a misguided salesman. "

He was driving at top speed to the Institute, where he had heard a fascinating speech several years before. The speaker was a preternaturally gifted international expert who touted his sales technique as the best in the world. That's just what our hero needed: the best sales strategy in the world. As he drove, he tried to remember the speaker's appearance.

He had been in his early 40s, tall, handsome, and charismatic. The speaker's name, however, eluded him. He was unconcerned about that; he could find out at the Institute. The one thing he did still remember was the man's title: StorySculptor.

Our hero was a bit embarrassed to remember that when he first encountered the StorySculptor he had not given the lecture his undivided attention. At the time, he was so successful on his own that part of him wondered if he really needed to hear this speech at all. By the end of the speech, however, he was convinced that the StorySculptor was a true sales expert. He remembered walking out to the parking lot with Carl, who had also been impressed. "Carl," he said, "if at any point in the future I ever get stuck and don't know what to do to keep my numbers up, tell me to remember the StorySculptor."

He gently turned his car into the Institute parking lot and nestled it in an empty space near the back. As he walked to the door, he smiled softly to himself and thought, *Thanks, Carl.*

2 The StorySculptor

Upon arrival, our hero learned that the StorySculptor didn't actually work for the Institute but was a valued business partner and frequently gave lectures there. Fortunately, the Institute's staff were happy to divulge his telephone number and call ahead to give our hero a proper introduction. Two days later, he met the StorySculptor in person.
"Please sit down," said the StorySculptor, gesturing to an overstuffed black leather chair in front of his mahogany desk. "What can I do for you?" Our hero cleared his throat. "Uh, yes, I am a successful salesman," he began. The StorySculptor nodded in encouragement. "Or, well, at least I was. I've started losing customers in droves, and nobody gives me concrete reasons for switching to my competitor's inferior product. I'm also having considerable difficulty

landing new customers. I have no idea what I'm doing wrong." His pulse quickened, and the burning in his face told him that he was blushing. It was embarrassing to admit that he needed so much help, but our hero also felt relieved to share his burden with someone who could help.

"Aha," said the StorySculptor, "another 'facts seller!'"
"Excuse me?"
"You're another 'facts seller!'"
Our hero was restless and growing uncomfortable.
The StorySculptor laughed. "I just mean that you know everything about your product to the smallest detail."
Our hero nodded enthusiastically.
"Absolutely."
"And you also know all about the competitors products and know the market inside and out?"
That sounded more like a statement than a question, but he answered, "Of course."
"And I know my colleagues and competitors in detail," he added. "How else could I expect to sell anything?"
"And now your customers are buying from your competitors but can't clearly articulate why they made the change." It wasn't a question.
Our hero nodded with a sad expression.
"How did you know?"
The StorySculptor seemed not to hear him.
"And prospective clients have started to procrastinate before signing your contracts, right? And in many cases you never hear from them again?"
"Yes! "
The StorySculptor chuckled.
"I understand you very well, and I can comfort you. You are not the first and will not be the last person to struggle with

this problem. In recent years and with the advent of advanced technology, many thousands of salesmen have come to me with the same problem."
"What does technology have to do with this?" Our hero wanted to know.
"Well, it has to do with the technology you are offering, and it has to do with the technique you are using to deliver it," replied the StorySculptor. "I also once sat where you are sitting now. Not physically, of course. I began my career in applied technology sales, and, just like you, I always wanted to improve. For a while, everything was great, but then I hit this frustrating wall. I got stuck there, and then I started to lose customers. I had studied and been trained in every possible sales technique: passive listening, active listening, and dozens more. But you know what? That somehow made it less and less fun. I realized that there was no point to investing all of that time and effort if it didn't help me acquire and retain customers. It got to the point where my health was suffering. I was expending so much energy trying to make sales that I completely burned out. I didn't want to do it anymore!"
As the StorySculptor related this honest and passionate tale, our hero felt himself drawn closer and closer. By the end, he was perched on the very edge of his seat, hanging on every word the StorySculptor spoke.
"So, I searched diligently for a solution, and have found the best sales method in the world."
Our hero's jaw dropped, but he didn't have time to say anything.
"The answer is...telling stories!"
Our hero faltered.
"Uh..." he stammered, "telling stories?"
"Haha! You should see your face," laughed the StorySculptor.

"It's the same face I made when I heard this for the first time. Nevertheless, it's true. Storytelling is the most successful selling method in the world!"
Our hero thought about this long and hard. His mentor did seem quite comfortable sitting there...and also quite successful. Perhaps this was the secret to his success. In any case, our hero wanted to know more. He remembered an old Chinese proverb:

He who asks a question is a fool for five minutes; he who does not ask a question remains a fool forever.

"Interesting," he heard himself say. "Could you explain this to me a little more?"

The StorySculptor was pleased. He could see this young man was now hooked, and he knew from experience that once his visitors understood the true power of storytelling, they were without exception more effective and happier salespeople. Their clients were increasingly enthusiastic, too.
"It's simple. Think about how children learn: through fairy tales! From Hansel and Gretel, they learn not to walk alone through a forest. Through Snow White, they learn the futility of vanity and malice. This is great news for sales professionals, who are truly not salesmen, but storytellers."

The StorySculptor took a framed poster in his hand that had been on his desk. When sitting behind the desk he could always see it. Now, he thought with a smile, it was time four our friend to see it.

He could read there in large letters:

Stories are the best selling tools in the world.

The StorySculptor continued: "In the end it is the story that sells because of the incredible staying power it has. It embeds itself deep into the subconscious of the listener and makes potential customers into enthusiastic brand and product ambassadors. What could be better?"

"Wow! Enthusiastic customers! Brand and product ambassadors!" thought our young friend. That was what he had always wanted. It was every salesman's dream. His reverie was broken by the voice of the StorySculptor.

"It is crucial that the sales story is well designed and effective. Whether you want to sell a product to a customer or an idea to an investor, a good story can make it happen. The best part is that it's simple enough for everyone learn." Our hero didn't hesitate.
"Can you teach me?"
"Well, I can guide you, and I can put you in touch with some other people who can help you, too. You will learn how the brain works as it relates to storytelling: You will experience the surprise of the opening, get to know the villain, learn how to leave a lasting impression, and, of course, how to seal the deal and make sales. It's a great comfort when you realize that selling is fun and that you can help satisfied customers enjoy the product or service you're selling even more. Furthermore, your customers will be enthusiastic ambassadors for you and your product and will provide valuable word-of-mouth advertising."

Yes, that was our hero's dream; it was exactly what he was looking for, down to the very last detail. He marveled that

the StorySculptor's technique was even working on him. He thought, *Whatever he's selling, I'm buying.*
"When does it start? What should I do?" he asked. "What seminars should I attend? How can I become a persuasive speaker like you? Can you recommend a strategy for handling objections?" The questions poured forth like a waterfall.
The StorySculptor laughed loudly and said, "So you think that you can convince your customers with rhetorical tricks?"
"Yes, because I have to tell them a convincing story! You just said so." Now our hero felt confused.

"Well, yes. You need something well-constructed and skillfully-told. But rhetorical tricks are unnecessary. These tricks and communication techniques are only necessary because ineffective salespeople believe that the customer doesn't truly want their product and will only buy it if tricked. And you know what? Well-trained salespeople achieve just that. You can motivate the customers with compelling and sophisticated rhetorical phrases: Most customers don't have the training to recognize that they're being plied with tricks, but you know exactly what the consequences are, yes?"

Our hero slumped in his chair. He hadn't expected the question and felt uncomfortable. He tentatively replied, "That the salesperson makes the sale...?"

The StorySculptor threw his hands up, exasperated. "Nonsense!" he cried. "He has created a lapse risk. The transaction is a sham, and if the customer realizes that in the ensuing days he's likely to call and cancel the sale. A friend or family member hears about the purchase and quickly convinces him that he doesn't really need the product or service, so he backs out of the contract."

Our hero had experienced this often, and he knew that many of his colleagues had also struggled with cancellation rates as high as 30 percent.

The StorySculptor continued his rant.

"And the customers who do not dare to cancel often do something far worse: They do not recommend you or what you're selling. They may even tell their friends and colleagues that they bought your product, but it wasn't very good. That, my friend, is the worst thing that can happen to you!"

Our hero had to concede that once again, the StorySculptor had hit the nail on the head. "Unfortunately, I've seen what you're describing many times before. That's what ultimately led to my current exasperation with all of this. I think that I will have to learn another approach."

"Exactly," replied the StorySculptor. "Once you learn this approach, you will no longer need rhetoric seminars, communication tricks, or strategies for overcoming objections. You'll give your customers a delightful experience and they will truly want your product. In fact, they will be so happy with it that they'll run to tell their friends and colleagues about it, too."

"You're right! That's what I want! Please help me achieve that." Our hero was now quite enthusiastic. " What must I do? "

And so it was that our hero began the exciting journey on which he learned the best selling method in the world. And that isn't all he learned...

The next stop for our hero was to meet Professor Susan Lombardi, as the StorySculptor had recommended a meeting with Professor Lombardi before doing anything else. He had called her assistant and had set up an appointment for today. Now he was on his way to her university.

3 Quantum Physics

Professor Lombardi was on the faculty for the local university's department of psychology and neurobiology. Our hero was nervous. Could he communicate with such an educated woman? Was he good enough? Just as he was beginning to drive himself crazy with such thoughts, the door opened and Professor Lombardi stepped into the room. She was an attractive woman in her early forties and wore a confident smile. She shook his hand.

"Hello! I'm Susan Lombardi. Nice to have you here."

Relieved, our hero introduced himself.

"The StorySculptor advised me to see you for help with my sales technique."

"Aha – for help with your sales technique," she nodded mysteriously. He looked puzzled at her and started feeling uncomfortable.

"Is there something strange about that?" he inquired.

"Well, nothing specific. It's just that yesterday somebody showed up here and wanted to learn specific techniques to manipulate the brain of his customers, but his problem was his product itself. It had so many features that it took literally hours to explain to a potential customer. His features list had hundreds of items to choose from. It just came back to me when you asked for help with your sales techniques"

"Don´t worry, the StorySculptor already told me that facts and figures don't sell at all. A story needs to be told and I'm here to learn how to create a compelling story that excites my clients. "

"Well, that's something very different. I'd be happy to help you. Tell me about your customers."

"Well, it's mostly senior executives. People responsible for making decisions from managers to directors and board members."

"I see." Professor Lombardi said as she leaned back in her chair and gestured to a framed photograph on a nearby table. She spun the frame so our hero could see it. It was a picture of a robot!

"No, no," he laughed. "No, I do not sell to robots."

"Good, then we've cleared that up. Now, tell me something. What makes people different than these metal boxes?"

"Well, we have emotions."

Professor Lombardi smiled. "Quite right. And we have a brain, which robots lack. They have an electronic memory, but not the rational and emotional intellect of a human. So if a computer program is able to analyze a potential sale on the basis of the delivery dates and on whether the product meets the necessary requirements, then the robot can calculate whether to buy or not. It's that simple."

Our hero listened with rapt attention. The professor continued:

"How is it, then, that people who use a computer for such calculations and comparisons reject your offer, even though your product clearly provides the best performance and meets all of their requirements perfectly?"

"This is exactly what frustrates me!" exclaimed our salesman. "I'll never understand!"

The professor took out another picture. It was a human brain. It wasn´t terribly nice to look at, but it was clearly a picture of a brain. She tapped it with her finger.

"This is why," she said. "It's very simple. The brain is the most complex and highly developed organ in our body. We only partially understand how it works, and we don't completely understand why it leaves us in a lurch sometimes. But we do know that it is highly efficient and that it always ensures the purposes of survival. Survival has both social and emotional components. These components are responsible for ensuring that your competitors sell, and you do not, even if your product is technically better."

Our hero listened in silence. It looked like she knew exactly what she was taking about and our friend was patiently waiting for her to reveal everything.

"We know that our brain is divided into two hemispheres. The part of our brain that handles analytical tasks is located in the left hemisphere; the emotions are processed in the right. The hemispheres are connected by a thick bundle of tissue called the corpus collosum, which robots don't have. It allows the two sides to communicate quickly with one another. Very efficient. "

"Which side of the brain is activated when you inundate your customer with data and facts?"

That question hit him. Of course it was the right hemisphere, he thought, which was attacked and needed to respond. But wasn't that a good thing? Didn't a seller want to convince a buyer with superior facts? Hold on a moment. Facts? Maybe not. He felt like he had just been split in two. One half shouted: No facts; stories!

The other was silent and couldn't find an answer. His insides were in a state of confusion, but he answered very carefully.

"Well, the left half," replied our hero. "Is that bad?"

Susan sensed a little shaking in his voice and smiled. This smile somehow put him at ease, and he couldn't help but find it intriguing. The walls around her office were filled with all sorts of academic titles and awards. He was aware that he was listening to a super sophisticated scientist on one count and to a great teacher on the other. But before he could sink any deeper into his own thoughts, she continued.

"Correct. Those who think logically and analytically use the left hemisphere of the brain, almost as if there was a computer in their skull. This presents a problem for the salesperson. Because the left hemisphere pays attention to facts and because it has been configured to be the dominant half to ensure our survival, it automatically searches for problems, lies, inconsistencies and negative details. This means that the analytical brain picks apart the first selling point, then analyzes the initial facts the seller offers, and it is so occupied in doing those things that it is incapable of truly hearing and evaluating the other points the salesperson makes. Therefore, the second or third wave of facts will be totally wasted."

This made sense. It was not necessary that he present all the facts and all the data because the client's brain was still busy with what he had said previously. It didn't matter how impressive his facts were; they were simply not being processed.

Lombardi continued her explanation.

"And if we manage to attract the customer's attention with the third argument, and force the brain to analyze it, then the first two arguments go unprocessed. Either way, most of the data and facts are totally lost. Plus, with this method we only address half of our customer's brain. And unfortunately, that part of the brain is not the part that tells the customer to buy anything!"

Our hero shook his head in amazement. He couldn't believe it. "Please continue. You have my undivided attention," he told her. She smiled.

"Do you remember being in school?"

"Of course."

"Was physics your favorite subject?"

"Hmm, huh, uh...not really, but I liked it more than most."

The professor chuckled.

"Haha, don't worry. Most people shy away from the natural sciences and mathematics. I, however, do not. So now we're going to dive a bit into the world of quantum physics. This is so exciting."

He looked puzzled and was wondering if he had suddenly been teleported into a Physics lecture. *Why in the world were they going to go into quantum physics now?* Our hero couldn't see how a discussion of physics could improve sales, but out of courtesy he smiled and agreed. *What was that all about?* he wondered.

"First people thought that the atom was indivisible. That's why they chose the name 'atmos,' the Greek word for "indivisible." Of course, scientists later discovered that the atom wasn't indivisible at all. Each atom has a nucleus orbited by electrons. Even the nucleus can be divided into protons and neutrons, and more recently physicists have discovered that even those particles can be divided! They are composed of quarks, and there are dozens of varieties. Then scientists learned that the proton and the neutron has a whole family of it's own, comprised of neutrinos, muons, tau neutrinos, muons and taus. Through an important discovery scientists just recently proved the existence of the higgs boson: A particle which was proposed over 40 years ago but was only detectable now utilizing super sophisticated technology called the LHR large Hadron Collider that they built for billions of dollars in Europe."

Our hero's head was spinning. He could not follow her. He felt so stupid and hoped fervently that she would stop, but she did not. On the contrary she sped up and threw more facts at him.

"Then there was the realization that these small particles don't behave like big clumps of matter - tables, cars, stones and so on. A stone's throw can be calculated exactly if we know its mass, shape, weight and the strength of the force behind the throw. Our left hemisphere is responsible for those calculations, by the way. Not so with the elementary particles, however, with the mesons, the bosons, and their ilk. With those, the laws of quantum physics take over."

Our hero was thoroughly confused. *Why would he calculate the path of a thrown stone? He wasn't even selling stones. Should he talk to his customers in quantum language?* He was confused but the professor lectured on. It looked like she was on a mission.

"An important contribution to the whole subject was Werner Heisenberg, a German physicist who formulated the Heisenberg Uncertainty Principle. According to Heisenberg, you cannot simultaneously know the location and speed of a particle.

Heisenberg discovered that the two complementary properties of a particle, for example the momentum and location, are arbitrarily determined simultaneously. The best-known example of two such properties are position and momentum. The Uncertainty Principle is not the consequence of the technical shortcomings of a measuring instrument, but of laws of quantum mechanics. Based on this principle, it is generally not possible to determine the location of a particle if you measure the electric charge as well. If you determine the location a particle you are unable to determine the electric charge. And that goes on and on with the impossible trial to measure two conditions

$$\Delta x \cdot \Delta p \geq \frac{h}{2\pi}$$

$$\Delta p \geq \frac{h}{2\pi \cdot \Delta x}$$

$$\Delta p \geq \frac{6,626 \cdot 10^{-34} Js}{2\pi \cdot 10^{-11} m}$$

$$\Delta p \geq 10^{-23} kgm/s$$

simultaneously at any given time. Best explained in his formula. He published it 1927. He was true genius!"

By this point, our hero was starting to panic. He felt completely lost and still had no idea what any of this had to do with sales. He felt like he was on a star in a far distant galaxy talking to an alien. He had to escape. He needed to get out of this. Why did he need to know anything about quantum physics? He was just a simple salesman.

"Excuse me, Professor..." he began hesitantly.

"Susan. Please call me Susan. After all, you come on the recommendation of my friend the StorySculptor. Please call me Susan."

Did she want to completely confuse him? Was she out to mock him? He was getting dizzy. He blurted out, "I don't get it. I'm sorry Susan, but I do not even remember what this is all about."

He was ashamed.

Susan laughed out loud.

Oh no, he thought. *She's going to kill me. I'm such a shameful disgrace.*

"So, was it a good sale or not?" she teased. "I gave you all of the facts, and every one of them is scientifically proven."

Oh great, now she was making fun of him. Or was she? His brain was spinning. He was starting to get the feeling that there was more to it.

She continued: "Somehow, though, my sales efforts failed. I have the best product; I can prove it, and yet my potential customers just stand there and stare at me. I feed their brains with perfect knowledge, but I'm not getting anything back."

All of the sudden something clicked in his brain. "Just like what happens to my clients when I feed them data."

"Exactly! Reciting facts doesn't lead to learning. It's like learning a language. Just learning the vocabulary isn't enough to speak. To speak you need to understand how these foreign words work together. But right before that you need to understand why you want to speak this language and how it will make you happy. If you want to sell something, you need the customer to learn what your product is all about, and why it will benefit them. Only then will your client understand why they need what you're selling."

"Aha," he heard himself say. She smiled.

"I've got help from a fellow who knows how to sell. Well, actually not really. He's a physicist, like me, but he's also a fantastic comedian and gives the Heisenberg Uncertainty Principle quite a different treatment than what I just gave you. Just to recap: Based on Heisenberg´s principle, it is not possible to determine the location of a particle if you measure the electric charge at the same time. If you determine the location of particle you are unable to determine the electric charge. And that goes on and on with the impossible attempt to measure two conditions simultaneously at any given time. However, when my friend explains it, he says:

"Imagine that you went with your assistant to a seminar in Chicago. Your wife knows where you are, but she has no idea what you are doing. Now imagine that in a few weeks your wife finds one of your dirty shirts with lipstick on the collar. Now she knows what you did, but not where you did it! Viola - that is the Heisenberg Uncertainty Principle!"

Our hero marveled. *When you put it that way, physics almost sound interesting.* Our hero smiled. She had just used this whole scientific lecture to illustrate her point. Facts don't sell because memorizing them is like memorizing a vocabulary list for school. Who would want to spend time cramming like that? People want to be entertained, to laugh, to enjoy themselves. When that entertainment also imparts knowledge, learning happens automatically and is lots of fun. Our hero made a mental note to tell Carl all about Heisenberg's Uncertainty Principle when he returned to the office.

"Isn't that a funny way to teach something to somebody?" a much friendlier professor asked. "I am very sure you can you can now teach the Uncertainty Principle to almost anybody else."

"Yes you're right. That is exactly what I just thought. I certainly will teach my colleague back in the office about the Uncertainty Principle later today. That's a very exciting way to teach."

Susan reached back, pulled out a card, and showed it to him

Facts bore!

Stories sell.

Facts distract!

Stories sell.

Facts confuse!

Stories sell.

He had to smile. "Thank you Susan! This was a great demonstration."

He now understood his fatal mistake: *Overwhelming his clients with facts and figures would only make them bored and distracted, just like what happened to him! Could it be that his more successful competitors were making sales by telling stories? Their products were clearly inferior, so they couldn't have won over their customers with cold, hard facts. If it only came down to the facts, it would be impossible for anyone to buy any product other than his. So if it wasn't the facts, it must be the story.*

"Wow! Where can I learn how to come up with stories like that? I mean, I'm not a comedian," he worried.

Susan smiled. "Not a problem. Everyone can learn. It isn't rocket science after all. We are all grateful to the StorySculptor, who has refined these techniques and helped salespeople to use them in every industry. A lot of it boils down to intuition, which he has studied and is now teaching it to anyone seeking advice and who wants to listen. It's all about learning the craft of storytelling. This is his passion. This is what he does, and I am personally very excited about it and love him for it."

"I'm confused. As a scientist, why would you ever have to sell anything?" He looked at her in surprise.

She laughed.

"Ha! Do you have any idea how expensive powerful femto lasers are? When our department needs new equipment, it's up to me to sell the university on that expense. Selling skills are useful to everyone, regardless of their job title. Our needs and ideas have to be sold to our partners, superiors, colleagues, children, and friends, always, anywhere, anytime..."

"...and we can do it more effectively if we pack those needs and ideas into a story!" our hero exclaimed enthusiastically.

Stories excite.

Stories stay.

Stories sell.

"Yes! Who would've thought you'd be this excited after a lecture on nuclear physics? Would you have ever thought that could happen before today?"

"Never," he replied. "This is incredible."

"Oh, no," Susan's iPhone beeped. She glanced at it and made a sad face.

"Please, go if you have to. Forget that I'm here," he suggested guiltily. She had spent almost an hour with him, and he knew from personal experience that time is money. He did not want to cost her money or aggravation.

"Well," she said, "that was my alarm clock. Unfortunately, my time is limited, and I have to go back to my bosons and mesons," she laughed.

Apparently he was unable to hide the look of disappointment that passed across his face. Still laughing, she said, "What´s the matter, young man? You look like you got hit by a truck!"

"Uh, uh ..." he stammered. "I feel like I have so much more I want to know..."

"I am sure you have a million questions. I did, too. You'll have all of your questions answered, although not by me. That's a quirk of the StorySculptor; he said that each of us should only explain part of the method: the part for which we are the specialists. The next person you need to meet is Kim Labonte, an excellent executive coach. I'll give you her contact information. Pay attention to what you hear there.

"Good luck on your little journey." With those words she stood up and gave him her hand. He jumped up, grabbed her hand, and started to thank her.

"It was my pleasure," she interrupted. "At the end of the journey you will meet the StorySculptor again and you, too, will become a StorySculptor. And this comes with a price." She smiled, turned around and floated out the door. She waved to him again before she finally disappeared for good and left him alone and befuddled.

Apparently he was unable to hide the look of disappointment that passed across his face. Still laughing, she said, “What´s the matter, young man? You look like you got hit by a truck!”

"Uh, uh ..." he stammered. "I feel like I have so much more I want to know...”

"I am sure you have a million questions. I did, too. You’ll have all of your questions answered, although not by me. That’s a quirk of the StorySculptor; he said that each of us should only explain part of the method: the part for which we are the specialists. The next person you need to meet is Kim Labonte, an excellent executive coach. I’ll give you her contact information. Pay attention to what you hear there.

“Good luck on your little journey.” With those words she stood up and gave him her hand. He jumped up, grabbed her hand, and started to thank her.

"It was my pleasure,” she interrupted. “At the end of the journey you will meet the StorySculptor again and you, too, will become a StorySculptor. And this comes with a price.” She smiled, turned around and floated out the door. She waved to him again before she finally disappeared for good and left him alone and befuddled.

Latte Macchiatto

Our hero needs his coffee, just like everyone else. After leaving Susan's office, he stopped at one of his favorite bars for a relaxing latte macchiato. He lingered there to drink it, and all sorts of interesting thoughts popped into his head. He thought about how dumb had he felt when the professor bombarded him with physics vocabulary. Although he had studied physics in school, albeit briefly, he had understood literally nothing except the beginning and end of her lecture. Was this the way his customers felt after hearing his sales pitch? Unlikely. After all, they were educated and experienced professionals who would be very difficult to confuse. They already understood exactly what he was selling, and they wanted facts and figures!

He took another sip of his macchiato, and then it hit him! He sat up abruptly, as if he had been struck by lightening.

Hmm, he thought. *Perhaps I'm selling to the wrong audience. So often I have to give sales pitches to managers and department heads, not the professionals who actually use my products. But if I'm peppering them with professional jargon, it's no wonder that they can't understand it.*

He sat on his stool and looked thoughtfully out into the street. *For a brief moment he thought he saw the people walking outside the café pause, turned around to him, and said, "but perhaps not."*

He brushed the thought aside and began to daydream. Surely, this was it! When he spoke to non-specialists (which always happened with new clients), he mistakenly used the same documents that he customarily presented to the experts. This virtually guaranteed that the non-specialists would miss most of the point, and would therefore be unlikely to arrange a second meeting between him and the experts.

That was probably the root of the problem, and the reason that his competitors were so much more successful than he was. Although his data depicted much better performance indicators, and his products used superior materials, making the downtime maintenance requirements less than that of the older materials the competitors were using. And that patented part with the .0674 performance indicator .... He stopped abruptly and couldn't help but laugh. There they were, the facts again. .0674 performance indicator! Like bosons and mesons!

He noticed a pretty redhead sitting to his left. He imagined himself striking up a conversation with her by saying,

Hello, my name is Bond...James Bond. I am six feet tall, weigh 160 pounds and have twenty grand in my checking account. I've been selling technical equipment for the past 28 months and live in a two-room apartment with my cat.

His grin widened. The redhead looked back at him, visibly irritated. This would probably have been the dumbest pickup line of his life...not to say that he'd enjoyed great success with any other pickup line he'd ever used...The truth was that both a lucrative sales career and a girlfriend had thus far eluded him. He told himself that it didn't much matter; he was too shy to approach a woman like that anyway.

He stared out the window as he negotiated with himself. By the time he turned around to face her, she was gone. He was momentarily angry with himself, but then he remembered that Susan had instructed to arrange a meeting with Kim Labonte. He rummaged in his pocket and found the scrap of paper containing her contact information. He dialed the number.

"Labonte," he heard a male voice say. "Good afternoon," he began, speaking with the most professional voice he could muster. Professor Susan Lombardi gave me this number and advised me to make an appointment with Ms. Kim Labonte.

"What is it about, then?" asked the voice.

"Well, I don't exactly know, to be honest. I was sent by the StorySculptor, who put me in touch with Professor Lombardi who has - how did she put it? - ah, passed the baton to Ms. Labonte."

"Sorry, but your story is a bit cryptic, and there are no women here named Kim Labonte. Please call again when you know what you want. Have a nice day." Then the man hung up.

What was that?

Our hero was too much of a salesman to simply accept defeat. He redialed the number. Again he heard the man's voice.

"Labonte "

"Yes, we were just disconnected. I would like to speak with Kim Labonte."

"That's me," the deep voice said.

It occurred to our hero that the voice had previously said that there was no woman named Labonte at that number. He chided himself for assuming that Kim was a woman's name.

"Oh, I thought that Kim was a woman."

The voice laughed now. "No problem. It happens all the time. Susan Lombardi recommended me, right?"

"Yes, and I met with her on the recommendation of the StorySculptor.

"Ah, the StorySculptor has quite the gift. He has helped us all improve our sales significantly." Mr. Labonte sounded much friendlier now. “And now you want to meet me and learn more about storytelling, right?"

"Yes, that would be great."

"How about next Wednesday at 3 p.m.?"

"That would be fantastic. I'll be there.”

“I'm looking forward to it."

4 About racing accidents

It was loud enough to burst the eardrums. The Formula 1 Ferrari hit the concrete wall almost head-on and disintegrated in a burst of flames and debris, followed by deafening silence.

Our hero stood in a large office. Four huge screens displayed a racing track, and small speakers pumped out the stentorian sounds of the race. The desk that dominated the room had a steering wheel bolted to it, and there were pedals nestled beneath it. The man who sat at the desk had his back to our hero. Another man stood behind him, screaming instructions.

“Left! LEFT!” he bellowed. Then came the crash.

"Too late." He concluded in a low soft voice.

Our hero didn't know what to make of all this. Kim Labonte's assistant had told him that he should go to the end of the hall and then into the left-most room. Now he seemed to be in some sort of huge Formula 1 simulator. He was just about to leave when the shouting man lowered his voice, which suddenly made him sound like Kim Labonte had on the telephone.

The tall, broad man turned around and smiled.

"Ah, hello. You must be the young man Susan sent who does not know what he wants."

"Uh, yeah. Hello," replied our hero. "Are you Mr. Labonte?"

"You're probably surprised to see me here in the middle of an Indy 500 race," laughed Labonte.

"And impressed by the technology that you have here."

"And the best part is that I can deduct everything from my taxes!" laughed the big man. Our hero remembered Labonte's brusque tone during his first phone call and chided himself for jumping to conclusions about him.

"By the way, this is Luigi. He's one of our race car drivers." He pointed to the chair, which was shaped like a race car seat. The occupant wasn't visible, save for an unruly crop of shiny black curls that sprouted above the headrest. It was fair to guess that Luigi had Latin roots of some sort, most likely Italian. This was quickly confirmed by Labonte:

"As a hot-blooded Italian he has, of course, chosen a Ferrari and, as you have just seen, smacked it into a concrete wall." He turned to the Italian.

"You're dead!"

Without turning around Luigi shot back:

"And your car is junk."

Our hero wondered what he was supposed to be doing here. He needed to improve his sales skills, not win an Indy car race. Nor, for the matter, did he need any lessons in how to kiss a concrete wall and never recover from the smooch.

Labonte was still speaking.

"I've already told you a thousand times: look where you want to go, not where the car is going. You're reacting a tenth of a second too late. You're turning left, so you need to look left. Don't obsess about an obstacle in front of you. Keep your eyes on the prize. These split-second decisions mean the difference between a crash and victory. Boom! You're dead and that beautiful car is a pile of high-tech scrap metal. "

The Italian muttered something like, "Yes, yes, it's fine. It'll be better next time." He swiveled his chair around and faced our hero. Labonte made a brief introduction, then rubbed his palms together.

"O. K., let's call it quits for today. You can try again next Thursday. I've got some business to attend to with our friend here."

Luigi waved and left the office, shutting the door softly behind him.

Our hero sat down and looked intently at the modeled IndyCar chair and the executive coach occupying it. Labonte leaned back.

"So," he began, “what brings you here?"

"The StorySculptor sent me to Professor Susan Lombardi, promising that she could help me improve my sales technique. By confusing me with her lecture on quantum physics, she helped me understand that facts don’t sell, but stories do. Once she had finished her bit, I was still eager to learn more, so Dr. Lombardi, in turn, referred me to you.”

"So what do you want from me?" asked Labonte smiling. “I know all about her special lecture on these tiny, shiny particles, and how much she enjoys to confuse new candidates on the way to master the best sales method in the world. So what can I do?”

"Well, I don’t quite know, but I have to sell more effectively than I have been. Something isn’t lining up, and my numbers are plummeting.”

"Why?"

"I think I'm caught in a sales traffic jam," our friend replied, hesitantly, “I have no idea why. My products are the best. The performance statistics don’t lie! I offer my clients a 30-nanosecond response time, a delay coefficient...”

"What?"

"A delay coefficient ... "

"What?" He interrupted again.

"A delay coefficient... "

"What is the point?" This was how Labonte had behaved on the phone. What was his problem?

Labonte didn't give our hero time to formulate a reply.

"Young man," he continued, "Susan has explained this to you. Facts are boring. You need to tell a story that inspires the subconscious and carries a clear message: buy my products and recommend it to the world!" The subconscious doesn't so much care about facts!"

"Delay coefficient... pffftt!" Labonte looked disgusted.

Our hero was embarrassed. His cheeks felt warm and he prayed that he would not blush like a nervous teenager.

"You're right. I'm probably falling into my old patterns. And I feel confused. Many of my clients are technical experts, and I don't think I should omit all of the facts and figures during my pitches. They're professionals! They want facts, figures, data, spreadsheets, you name it! And rightly so! You can't build a winning IndyCar if the technical specifications are wrong. If the ceramic discs don't compensate for the performance of the negative maximum delay, the brakes fail and people get injured." When I'm selling to technical experts, I can tell them entertaining stories until I'm blue in the face and still not make a sale." Our hero froze, pleased with himself for giving slight resistance.

Labonte smiled. "You're right. Luigi can sing you a song about what happens when the brakes fail," he chuckled. "Whom do you sell to in most cases?"

Our hero was thrilled. He was right! He straightened up and went on.

"I sell to manufacturers of engineered components for the automotive and aerospace industries. Other industries also use our products."

"And when you make a sales pitch, who do you usually speak to?"

"Mostly technical experts from existing clients and management representatives from clients I'm hoping to acquire."

"And new acquisition is the weak point at the moment," interjected the executive coach.

Unfortunately, it was true. Our friend felt his heart sink again.

"How do you know that?"

"Well, you were visiting the StorySculptor and he has sent you on a journey. This means you're stuck, and you yourself just admitted that you have a turnover problem. You clearly know your products very well and have all of the data that proves their superiority when compared to competing products. Technical experts will understand those dense mountains of data, so obviously your problem is with the non-technical types. These 'dumb managers,'" he said, making quotation marks with his fingers in the air.

"Let me guess," he continued, "You use the same presentation for all contacts and convey the exact same content, right? And you know that presentation inside and out. Even if I dragged you out of bed at 3 a.m., you could still give me a perfect, professional presentation, right?"

Our hero nodded vigorously.

"Of course. You could call me at any time of the morning, noon, or night, and I could deliver the perfect sales pitch, even straight from bed. I've got it down to a science." The answer shot from our hero's mouth like the bullet from a gun. He was proud of himself...for a second.

"Says the man who comes up empty handed every time he tries to sell anything."

Our hero resisted the urge to throttle the larger man. He took a deep breath to calm himself. Labonte was right, after all. Again.

"Yeah, but..."

"Young man," interrupted Labonte, "do you know what the Cheshire Cat said to Alice when she asked him which way she should go?"

What kind of a question was that? Alice in Wonderland? Then he caught himself. Oh, a story. Of course.

"No, I don't," he replied.

The cat asks Alice where she is going and she tells him that she doesn't know. Do you know what the cat says?"

Our hero shook his head.

He tells her that if you don't know what your destination is, it doesn't matter what path you take. You'll always wind up somewhere."

Our hero remembered the abrupt end to his first conversation with Labonte.

Call back when you know what you want, he had said.

The formerly mystifying words suddenly made sense to our hero. He understood!

You have to know whom you want to sell to. That determines how you sell it.

"I understand," he gushed, "I need to know who I want to sell something to and base my approach on that! I mean, I need to use a different story for different people."

Labonte was visibly pleased.

"Exactly," said the happy giant, "in sales, there's no such thing as 'one size fits all.' The rules of storytelling apply at any level and are essential for success, but you have plenty of options as to how you present the story. For example, experts can handle a more fact-intensive sales pitch than someone without technical expertise. It's like cooking. Sometimes you need to spice it up and give it a Cajun taste and sometimes you need to keep it basic.

"To understand which dish, eh, story we need to make the sale, we first need to determine what we want to sell to whom. This is called the "outcome frame." Use the wrong story, or no story at all, and you're setting yourself up to fail." Labonte leaned back and stretched his arms over his head.

“The art of selling begins before selling. It begins by determining your outcome frame, because you need that in place to build an effective story.”

"Do you remember Luigi and the Ferrari accident? Luigi didn’t look at where he was going because he was preoccupied with getting there. At racing speeds it only takes a millisecond to smash into the barrier. The top drivers in the world understand this. No one sees the concrete wall. They see their destination. Because they know where they want to go, where they need to slow down, where they must speed up, and where they can overtake. They have to know all of those things for every race they compete in.”

Labonte stood up, took off his suit jacket and folded it neatly over the back of his chair. Sitting down, he continued.

"And that's the difference between success and happiness. You’re like Luigi. He never is prepared for the race. You drive off to your sales pitch and talk to the track manager about the delay coefficient, but he only knows how to speak in terms of track conditions. Delay coefficients only make sense if you pitch to a mechanic. Using the same pitch for everyone is like driving with the wrong tires on a wet track. Before long, you go boom!”

He clapped his hands. "Crash, no sale!"

Labonte had hit the nail on its head. Our hero had reams of sales documents and presented without considering the goals of his pitch. Sometimes he didn't know who he would be pitching to until he arrived on site. Invariably, he would begin his pitch and realize soon thereafter that the manager was no longer paying attention to what he was saying. With the manager disengaged, BOOM! No sale, just as Labonte said.

"This makes sense, and now I know what I need to do better. Thank you for opening my eyes. I will start changing my technique today: facts out, stories in, adjusting the spices levels for my audience."

"Are you sure that you know how and where to spice things up? Do you know how to build a story that really sinks in and sells the product?"

"Uh...not really. But I learned something very important."

"And what would that be? " laughed Kim Labonte.

Before you start selling to anybody, you need to understand who you are selling to.

Then you need to tailor the story for that specific audience: A story which sinks in, sticks, and sells.

"Now I just need to learn how to develop the stories, but I'm confident that the StorySculptor has sent me on this journey to ensure I meet the people who can teach me." He smiled at the giant.

Labonte rested his elbows on his desk blotter and clasped his hands.

"So it is, but do not forget that at the end of your journey- when you hit the StorySculptor again- this will come at a price."

Susan Lombardi had told him the same thing, and our hero was suddenly starting to think that this didn't sound too good.

Labonte stood up and clapped a hand on our hero's shoulder.

"And now we're going for a drive. How about a few rounds in the IndyCar?"

Our hero felt Labonte push him in the direction of the simulator. When he got close, he saw there were multiple cockpits.

A special presentation

Instead of dry data, our hero now had a Jaguar. A Jaguar?

It was still early. Eight o'clock and our hero was prepared. In an hour, he would be visiting a potential customer, and he was excited to try out his new, improved presentation.

He'd done some research and learned that his contact with the company had a degree in biology. A smart man, to be sure, but not an engineer. To adjust, our hero cut most of the dry facts out of his materials and added a picture of a sleek Jaguar. Not the luxury car, but a mighty, black, muscular cat. Of course, our hero also packed his complete "normal" presentation, complete with data sheets and graphs. He was prepared on every front. He even had time for a quick cappuccino at his favorite coffee shop.

As he sipped his drink, the redhead walked (no, floated) in. She went straight to the counter, ordered, paid, and left. Our hero asked himself if he was day-dreaming. Probably not. She probably lived or worked nearby. He told himself that he would come back until he saw her again and be prepared with a special presentation to impress her. He chuckled to himself. He'd probably be more like a jaguar, slinking around behind her until she left the building. He finished his cappuccino and headed to his appointment.

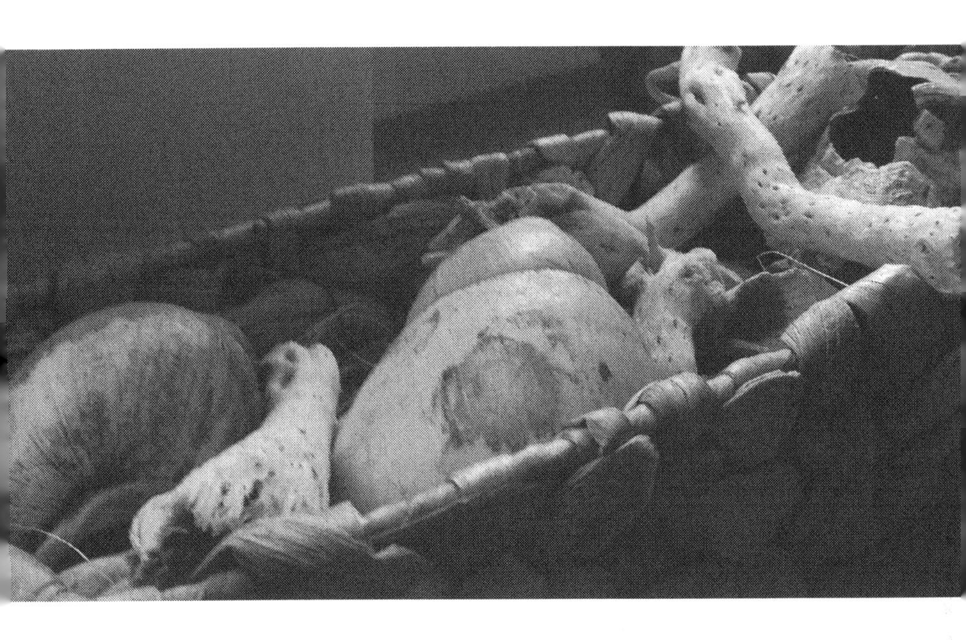

5 Glibbergummi

The hallway was dark: With the door behind him closed, it was almost totally devoid of light. An emergency lamp flickered to life above his head. He remained enveloped in shadows. "Welcome," bellowed a deep voice. It seemed to come from everywhere at once.

Our hero gasped as a man leapt in front of him. He seemed to actually come out of the wall. He cackled loudly and dissolved into a fit of giggles.

"Welcome!" he said. "Welcome to Ghosts and Monsters. We build haunted houses."

More lights flicked on, illuminating a pink, gelatinous blob that grabbed weakly at our hero, then seemed to collapse in on itself. Our hero clutched his chest and prayed that this was all simply a nightmare.

He heard another voice. It sounded more human than the first.

"Don't worry," said the voice, "they won't hurt you. They just want to play." A man stepped into the opposite end of the hallway and strode purposefully down to our hero, extending his hand in welcome.

"I'm Tom Schneider," he continued, "and we build the best haunted houses in the world!"

"Well, those things back there sure gave me a fright"

"All in good fun," Schneider reassured him. "As I said, they just want to play!"

He led the way down the hallway and into a room that looked like Frankenstein's laboratory. Body parts, skeletons, bats, bugs, and monster parts were strewn around the room, taking up every available flat surface. They were fakes, to be sure, but the most convincing props our hero had ever seen.

Schneider offered our hero a chair and sat down behind his desk. He picked up a remote control and pressed a button, causing a flat-panel TV screen to fold out from the opposite wall.

"Let's have another look at that, shall we?" He pressed play, and our hero saw himself on the monitor, scared out of his mind by the darkness, strange voices, and pink blob. He had to laugh at how silly he looked. It was kind of funny, now that he wasn't in the middle of it.

"I can't help it, but I have the suspicion that you're good friends with monsters, aren't you?" our hero said smiling.

"I sell all sorts of scary stuff," explained Tom Schneider. "Mainly interior decoration for haunted houses and theme parks. I love to shock my customers, just like I did to you. That way they experience our products and see how scary they can be. There's nothing like a startled customer."

"Interesting. You sell things by scaring people. That's a new one for me. The StorySculptor, Susan Lombardi, and Kim Labonte hadn't mentioned frightening techniques."

Schneider laid the remote on his desk.

"Ah, yes. The StorySculptor's clique! I am usually the third person the Master's little piglets come to see. People like you, who want to understand how selling really works."

"Yes, Mr. Labonte has recommended that I visit you and said that you will surprise me for sure. And you've succeeded completely. I can see now how perfect your method is for your business because your customers get to experience what you sell. But I can't use this approach. I'm not selling any monsters."

"Well, I'm sure killing your customers with facts is just as bad as attacking them with monsters. Ha!"

He cracked his knuckles.

"The giant, Labonte, must have told you that, huh?" our friend concluded.

"He didn't have to. The problem is that all of you "story-beginners" are approaching it wrong. You go to a meeting, bring out your presentations, and dive right in to complicated, technical details that leave most of the audience confused and bored. Two hours later, a competitor comes in with a flashy story and seals the deal."

"Yes, that's true," agreed our friend, "but I have started making improvements. Just yesterday I used a jaguar to make a point about delay coefficients to a non-specialist. I explained that jaguars catch their prey because they are capable of quick stops, quick starts, and they have the ability to quickly change direction while running."

He thought back to that sales pitch. *He'd begun well, but slipped into his old habits until he noticed that two of the three managers were losing interest. To get them back on track, he showed them three video clips of jaguars running and hunting, and explained the product in those terms. By the end of the meeting, two of the tree managers had approved the pitch and agreed to set up a meeting with their technical director.*

Voila! He had already won a stage victory. He beamed at Tom, whom he had already begun to refer to as "Mr. Monster" in his thoughts.

The monster applauded.

"That's quite a big step. Congratulations."

"Thank you, I feel great about it, and I am very grateful to the StorySculptor, the professor, and the giant for what they helped me achieve. Now I'm curious as to what I'll learn next."

Mr. Monster leaned back and pursed his lips. "I was hoping that you had already caught that?"

He looked puzzled.

“Do you know why I scare my customers?”

“I thought you said it was to prove that your products were scary.”

“Sure, but there’s another reason. Any guesses?”

Our hero shook his head.

“It’s a strong opening. When they come in, they immediately feel the fear from our products running up their spines, which instantly grabs their attention. If you don’t have someone’s attention from the very beginning of your sales pitch, you’ve already lost. Strong openings are also great in last-minute situations in which you need to make a sale with little or no preparation time.”

“But I don’t work in the horror industry.”

Mr. Monster chuckled.

“The strong opening is intended to ensure that the potential customer directs his attention to you, he isn’t distracted, and he is really interested in what you’re going to reveal next."

Yes, ok, that works in your business, but only with horror goods, otherwise not. How do you scare someone with ERP software or with car accessories or cell phone plans? "

Tom laughed. "With cell phone plans you only have to hear the price, and that certainly scares you. But seriously, fright is only one form of strong opening. The strong opening is intended to ensure that the potential customer's attention is focused on you and your offer. You want him undistracted and ready to see what kind of interesting goodies you've got in store for him."

Without waiting for a reply, Schneider barged ahead.

"Let me give you another example. In Hollywood, a movie director named Peter Gruber was looking for his next film. He requested an appointment with Terry Semel, the head of Warner Bros. Semel agreed to see him, but Gruber knew he would only have a few minutes for his pitch. Ordinarily, it would have been better to reschedule the meeting for a later date, but Gruber didn't have that kind of time. He knew that he needed to impress the producer from the minute he walked in the door. Gruber also had another problem. A few years earlier, Semel had produced a box office flop. It had been a disaster for the studio, especially because the thing had gone over budget in production. The main characters were similar to those that Gruber had developed for this project, and the director was now worried that the similarity might cost him the contract."

Our hero sat uneasily in his chair, eager to learn what happened.

"Gruber only had one chance with Terry Semel, so he needed a strong, no-fail opening. So you know what he did? He ran right into Semel's office and yelled, 'Terry, your family has been slaughtered!'"

Our hero did a double take.

"So of course Semel freaked out, and guess what? Gruber had Terry's undivided attention for the rest of his pitch."

Our hero shook his head.

"Semel bought it and ended up producing Gorillas in the Mist, which turned out to be a huge hit for Warner Bros. He knew he had to sell that movie in minutes and to do it in a way that would not remind Semel of his previously failed project. It was a film about Tarzan where they had unsuccessfully put stunt men in gorilla suits, making gorillas a sensitive topic in Semel's world. However, having a strong opening landed Gruber that film deal."

Mr. Monster stood up and took a sip of his coffee. The mug looked eerily like a human skull.

"If you learn one thing from me, learn this:

A strong opening is key to every sales pitch you make, regardless of your audience or what you are selling.

Our hero raised an eyebrow.

“But what about technical equipment? Surely I don’t need a strong opening for that, right?"

“Wrong! You always need something to focus your audience’s attention and make them curious about your product. Something which grabs their undivided attention; something which refocuses them and make them forget about everything else going on around them.”

“So what if I gave everyone a candy bar beforehand? Would that be a strong opening?” He felt silly even asking that question. Mr. Monster laughed.

“Well, if they have a sweet tooth you might make a sale. But the most effective strong openings are connect your client to what you’re selling.”

He took another sip and plunked his mug down on his desk.

"A simple technique for the strong opening is to talk about another client’s experience which ultimately leads to a question or a call to action for this customer. For example, one of my friends is selling a system that allows users to send documents securely to mobile devices. At the beginning he tried to explain all of the benefits of his product, but he didn’t make much progress. Then he switched to the tactic I’ve just described. His modified sales pitch began like this:

„Last week, a clerk auditing a Fortune 500 company accidentally sent an internal balance draft to the wrong email address. The file ended up with a journalist from the Chicago Tribune. This cannot happen with PadCloud."

Our hero nodded excitedly. He could see how such a pitch would be immediately appealing to corporate executives, as they would want to avoid such a data breach at all costs. "Why don't you try to use your jaguar in a strong opening," Tom suggested. "I'd like to hear it."

Our hero quickly gathered his thoughts.

"Do you know what happens when a jaguar – the cat, not the car – can't slow down quickly enough?"

Mr. Monster was mute.

Our hero felt his stomach churn. "Not good?" he asked.

"Ah, oh, sorry, were you expecting an answer?" Tom looked at him questioningly.

"Yeah, that's the whole reason I asked in the first place," he replied indignantly.

"Well, that's not ideal. Questions are okay, but questions can quickly make your presentation go off the rails. If you confuse your audience or make them uncomfortable, you run the risk of losing them. Try using rhetorical questions in your opening. I mean questions you don't really expect an answer to."

"Got it." Our hero cleared his throat and made a second attempt.

"You know what happens when a running jaguar can't slow down quickly?"

He didn't wait for an answer.

"They starve to death because they can't catch their prey. Slowing down – braking, if you will – is what keeps them alive. They need to be able to find prey, chase it, make quick right and left turns, perform u-turns, even 360s, just like the prey the big cat is chasing down. Without quick turns there will be no food: There will be starvation. It's the same thing with our product, which tailors your business to current market conditions and can perfectly follow the direction the market takes. This precision and flexibility means that you'll never starve for lack of sales."

Schneider gave our hero a thumbs-up.

"Wonderful. This is nice. If this strong opening is suitable to your product it will be surely different from what your competitors are doing. Of course, it would be even better to customize your opening for each intended audience. You can use your outcome frame to choose an opening and direct the rest of your sales presentation, too."

Our hero nodded eagerly, encouraged by the praise.

"Could you give me another example? That would be really helpful." He realized that maybe Schneider would think he was slow on the uptake, asking so many questions, but he didn't care. He was learning!

He was thinking of the old Chinese proverb:

He who asks a question is a fool for five minutes; he who does not ask a question remains a fool forever.

Schneider smiled and nodded.

“Sure. Let’s talk about Hollywood. When was the last time you went to the movies, and what film did you see?”

This was an easy question. Our hero had recently seen the latest James Bond film...alone, with no girlfriend, but Schneider didn’t have to know that part.

“Two or three weeks ago. The new James Bond Film.”

“Do you remember how the movie started?” asked Schneider.

“Yeah, there was this crazy chase scene with a bunch of explosions and special effects. The whole audience was on the edge of their seats!”

"What, no opening title sequence and catchy music? Bond Movies are famous for those.”

"Yes,” replied our hero, “but only after the chase scene. Then the audience could relax...” then it hit him. “Wait a minute!"

He sat up straight, energized down to the tips of this toes.

“A strong opening!” Schneider smiled approvingly. “Hollywood demonstrates how to grab someone’s attention and hold on to it. The entire theater was totally focused by the end of that chase scene.”

"Calm down, young man," laughed Tom. "You're right! Think about how many times you’ve seen that technique used in films, and to great effect. It makes Hollywood hundreds of millions of dollars every year, and it's ideal for us salespeople too."

Still excited our hero nodded profusely.

"Enough for today," said Tom, glancing at his watch. "My next customers are due any minute now. Now that you've experienced my strong opening, it's time to take a ride on my private ghost train! It's just around the corner."

Our hero felt terrible, but he wore the smile of the someone in the know, somebody who knew that he was on the upswing, that he was learning how to sell better than anybody else. He was already looking forward to learning the next step in this marvelous system. He was so excited, in fact, that even the thought of a ghost train didn't faze him.

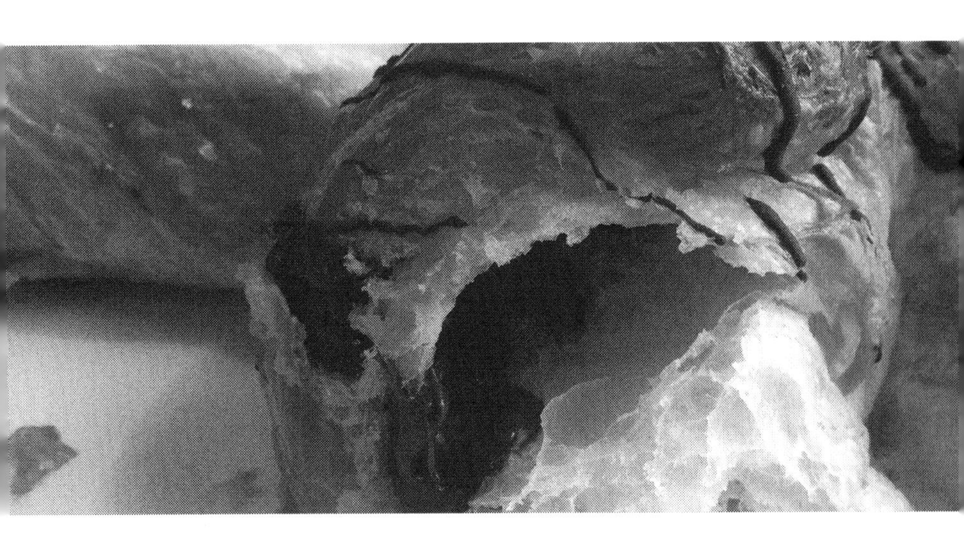

Chocolate croissant

Our hero was back at his favorite café. He sat alone with his thoughts, nibbling on a chocolate croissant and sipping a latte macchiato. The best coffee in town. *That's why I'm here*, he told himself. *Well, at least officially.*

He couldn't help but wonder if the beautiful redhead would walk in, but then he realized the thought of her suddenly arriving scared him more than Mr. Monster's scary props.

He took another bite of his croissant. Could a strong opening help when flirting?

He chided himself for not thinking of this before. Of course it could! Why not? The objective was the same, right? Sell products, or sell yourself. Same thing, in a way. In both cases you want to come out ahead of the competition and hold someone's attention long enough to make them interested in you.

And at this point it was essential for him to differentiate himself from his competitors with their tans and rock-hard muscles.

Our hero let his mind wander. How the heck could he do that?

I could pour my latte on my shirt, he told himself, then immediately chided himself for having such a stupid idea. He chuckled and took another sip, drumming his fingers on the table. He needed a strong opening that he could deliver even while nervous or distracted. After all, he knew that if he wasn't adequately prepared; all of his thoughts would get hopelessly jumbled together the minute the redhead looked at him.

So, that was it. He just needed a strong opening. Then he would be prepared.

Hey, why shouldn't he use the techniques he learned from the StorySculptor and his team to flirt? It was somehow a sale, wasn't it? He was selling himself to another person. The thought had come to him once before when he had seen her for the first time.

He vaguely remembered his introduction: *I'm 5`10, weigh 87 kg and have 12,865.14 dollars on my account. I sell technical equipment and have been on the job for 28 months*...something like that.

Pretty lousy. Mr. Monster's strong opening had a little more flair to it. So it was decided: He needed a strong opening.

6 Breakfast with the Italian

The redhead had not appeared, but our hero had used the time wisely. After all, thinking of strong openings was a good use of his time for all sorts of reasons. After giving up on the idea that the redhead wasn't going to waltz through the door, he sighed and checked his watch. He had an appointment with Luigi, whose phone number Mr. Monster had produced only after making him suffer through another monster show on his way out. And that was literally all he'd given him: a string of digits and the name "Luigi" scrawled in red pen. The man on the other end of the line had a strong Italian accent and had immediately offered to have breakfast the following morning at 8 a.m. Good for business, yes, but that meant our hero would have no time to swing by his café that morning to check for that beautiful redhead. He comforted himself with the notion that he would check on his way back from breakfast.

He stood at Luigi's front door and pressed the bell. Luigi Lombardi was written on the nametag. It was six floors up, but it felt he was climbing Mount Everest. Our hero was flushed and wished fervently for a handkerchief to mop his brow.

How do you just forget to install an elevator?!

The door flew open to reveal a tiny, smiling man with curly black hair. He made an inviting gesture and disappeared into the apartment, giving our hero no choice but to follow. He saw another figure move in the back of the apartment. He thought he recognized them but wasn´t sure. It was one of those diffuse feelings. Interesting... As he heard the click of high heels on the tile floor our hero knew who it was.

Dr. Susan Lombardi was apparently on her way out the door, fully dressed with a mahogany briefcase in hand. She smiled and waved.

"Good morning! Nice to see you again. I hope you're well. Luigi will take good care of you!" She turned to Luigi as she opened the front door. "Bye honey! Gotta go. I'm late!" And she disappeared out the door.

Luigi, not to be outdone, addressed the closed door:

"Ciao, Bella, you star in my eyes, don't leave your poor Luigi alone for too long! Come back soon, my dearest!"

A true Italian. Ever dramatic.

So. Luigi Lombardi. Professor Susan Lombardi. Lombardi! How had he missed that? Susan's husband, of course.

"Come in come in come in!" chirped Luigi. "You'll wear out the door mat, eh?" Our hero smiled and followed him through the short hallway and into the kitchen.

"Thanks. I was just surprised to see Professor Lombardi here!"

Luigi laughed loudly.

"Ha! I 'd be surprised if she *wasn't* here in the morning, know what I mean? After twenty years of marriage. Ha!"

Luigi rummaged happily in a cabinet as he continued.

"You have the same journey behind you as a lot of other people we've had in this kitchen. They start with the StorySculptor, then off to Susan, before she sends them to our good friend Kim Labonte-"

"Wow! That was you! You crashed the Ferrari!" exclaimed our hero, before catching himself. "Uh, sorry, I mean you had that...terrible accident," he continued.

"No, no," laughed Luigi, "That was definitely a wreck. The great Enzo Ferrari forgive me! But thank God that the Ferrari was just on the computer screen, right?"

Lombardi was on a roll. He didn't wait for a response.

"So! You learned about outcome frames from Kim, and then you got scared silly at Tom Schneider's before he gave you the scoop on strong openings, right?"

"Exactly," said our hero. "It's fascinating stuff and I'm grateful to all of you for helping me learn so much. At this point, I'm wondering what more I'll even be able to learn from you. Some other building block to the perfect sales story, I'm sure, but what? "

Luigi gestured for him to take a seat at the large kitchen table, covered with an abundance of fragrant breakfast foods. He spotted the coffee pot and nearly squealed with delight. *Thank God for caffeine!*

"Well, what can I say? The beginning of every sales story is tremendously important. Think of it like the turbo. As a racecar driver that's how I think of it, at least. Without it, the story is flat and boring. With the right beginning, however, a story can be great! It gets inside you and stays in your subconscious, where it remains for a long time. It's so important for it to sink in and stay there for a long time, in your customer's subconscious, that is." He buttered a slice of toast.

"Ever heard of Dr. No?"

"Of course. He's a villain from the James Bond films." This was familiar ground for our hero. He knew everything about Bond. James Bond. He knew the stories, the characters, and all the cast. He even knew some historical data and some rarely known facts. And of course he knew Dr. No.

"Right. Now try this exercise. Close your eyes and try to see the Bond films in your mind. Call up the scenes with Dr. No."

That was a no brainer for him. Our hero sat there, eyes dutifully closed, and called up the mental image of Dr. No, letting the scenes play in his mind. Hey! Hold on. How did the redhead enter the scene? She came in and was trying to distract him a bit. No, not now honey! he almost heard himself say, but thankfully managed to control it. He managed to send her away for the time being and refocused on this Bond story with the dangerous Dr. No. He transported himself to the cinema where the action played in front of him on the big screen. It felt exciting and relaxing at the same time.

“Hey, do not fall asleep!" His eyes flew open at the sound of Luigi’s voice. The Italian laughed merrily. "No, no, it's okay. I can see that you have very vivid memories. That’s a good thing. Now, we are going to actually change the course of the Bond film in your head. Are you ready?"

Our hero nodded and closed his eyes again, quickly immersing himself back in the world of James Bond.

"Remove Dr. No and any other villain from the movie."

He opened his eyes.

"Do what? The movie doesn’t make sense without a villain.” *What’s this guy want Bond to do? Go play golf or something? Or just go straight to seducing those beautiful Bond girls? That might be interesting, but not the kind of film they show in a regular cinema.*

Luigi grinned widely.

"Boring? Oh. And how do most sales presentations go? Do they have a hero and a villain, or just James Bond playing golf for an hour?

Our hero was speechless. Luigi was right.

Most sellers presented a predictable litany of facts. It was like monotonous golf commentary, he admitted. *He takes his 5-iron, and hits down the fairway. The ball comes down right on the approach. Now it looks like he's going to use his chipping wedge and manages to land it one meter in front of the hole. He comes up short on his first put, but sinks his forth for par. Four shots on a par 3 hole. Ugh! He was boring himself.*

How was that even possible?

"Most sales pitches are like a Bond film in which Bond does nothing but play golf. It's boring! Nobody remembers anything by the end. There's nothing funny, nothing interesting, nothing to take away or think about later. And that is perhaps the most important thing. No one is going to retell a boring story. We want our customers to find our stories so inspiring that they tell their friends and acquaintances. As those stories are all about you and your product, those friends and acquaintances learn to associate your products with the excitement of those stories!"

Luigi was on a roll.

"Think about what happens when you see a movie. You can't wait to talk about it! *'Hey, have you seen the new Bond film? It's awesome! At the beginning, Bond steals a motorcycle out of an alleyway and then gets into this crazy chase, and it seems like everyone in the city is following him!'* From that description alone, you can't wait to see this movie for yourself. That's what we want to achieve: We want to get our customer talking about our products and services. If a moviegoer leaves in the middle of the film or comes close to falling asleep, he's not going to say anything about the experience, at least nothing positive. Or even worse, if someone asks him about it he's likely to say, 'It was a flop. Save your money and stay home.'"

"Exactly!" cried our hero. "I want my customers to be thrilled and tell others about my products. I want to have them sitting on the edge of their seats, waiting for the next piece of action. But how can I do that? Obviously I need a strong opening, but that's just the beginning. I can't just pull gags for the entire presentation, can I? There's no real content there. I don't want to just distract my audience, so they don't learn any real information about what I'm selling."

What was this other thing? Full of expectation, he looked at Luigi.

Luigi nodded.

"Exactly. Too much action is not the solution, and confusing plots aren't helpful either. I began my career as a playwright, and then I transitioned to writing screenplays. For a long time, Susan and I lived together very happily, each of us with our own career. Then she learned the storytelling method, and she helped me master it. At that point, we realized that Susan's career – neuroscience – explains why hammering customers with a barrage of facts is actually counterproductive in sales. On the other hand, I was able to write stories that better captured people's emotions and kept them talking long after they left the theater. One night we went to the theater with the StorySculptor, and afterwards we came back here for a nightcap. We sat at length and discussed the philosophy and psychology of sales, and how storytelling plays a critical role. We talked about the most important element in a good stage play, too. Susan and the StorySculptor spoke heatedly about the need for strong openings with simple language, short sentences, and the presence of the entire ensemble. I sat there and had my fun as they went around and around, the scientist and the sales master himself, both experts in their fields but missing one crucial element! Finally, I couldn't stand it anymore and jumped in saying in my most portentous voice, of course, "Without the Wicked Witch, nothing works."

"There was dead silence. They both looked at me as if I'd fired a rifle. Then the StorySculptor jumped up and shouted, "Luigi, that's it! This is the missing element! This is what makes the difference between a good and a bad movie or a good and a bad pitch! The evil witch!" He danced around like a little kid on Christmas. Even Susan was thrilled. That evening I unintentionally elevated sales to an entirely new level. Since that night, the StorySculptor's technique has been even more effective."

Our hero was amazed. *The wicked witch?*

"So you need an ugly old women with a hooked nose and a face full of warts?"

"Exactly," laughed Luigi, "and above all, they must fly around on a broom." He cackled with delight. Our hero had the distinctly uncomfortable feeling that Luigi was laughing at him. His cheeks began to burn.

"Young man, the wicked witch is only one possible villain. Think about it. In the Bond franchise, Dr. No is just one of the many villains, and every good story has one. Even a romance is boring if there's no antagonist. You can't have a thriller without a killer! What would Sherlock Holmes be without Moriarty? Special agent Gibbs from NCIS would have to sit around playing snooker all day if they didn't have any dead bodies popping up. All the CSI guys from Las Vegas, Miami, and New York would be out of work and would be sent to the unemployment office. No single movie or TV series would work."

Luigi simulated a yawn. A long yawn.

"This makes sense to me in theory, but how can I use it for selling technology? I'm not selling wicked witches and Dr. Nos."

"It's not about the villain as a person *per se*. It is about the emotional distance between what can happen and what *cannot* happen if we use product A versus product B. The villain doesn't have to be a person. It may be a *circumstance*, a side effect, some imminent danger, or something that happens to their competitor because they didn't use your product. It is only important that you create an emotional difference between the two. This is how the story gets its sticking power."

Our hero suddenly felt like he was starting to get it. Emotional distance. Get the customer to feel the danger, and the solution seems much more attractive. If you don't know the risk, then you can't really identify and assess the value of the product offered. That was logical, but he'd never thought of it that way before. In his standard sales pitch, he stressed the benefits of his products, but failed to show why his audience was going to have problems living comfortably without them. There was no sense of urgency, and no emotional depth. No flying witches. But wasn't he on the right track now with his Jaguar story?

"Luigi, since my visit to Mr. Monster I've been busy perfecting my strong opening. I even had a successful dry run with it!"

Luigi raised his eyebrows.

"Mr. Monster?"

Oops.

"Yeah, I guess I've got nicknames for each of the StorySculptor's friends. I call your wife *The Professor*, Kim Labonte is The Giant because he's so tall, and Tom Schneider is *Mr. Monster,* since he's so scary."

"What about me?" Asked Luigi.

"Well, I'd like to call you *Italiano* if that's okay."

Luigi clapped his hands in delight.

"What a great honor! Of course! I would be happy for you to call me...*Il grande Italiano!*" The tiny Italian giggled and gulped his rapidly cooling coffee. "Now! Back to your strong opening. You were saying?"

Our friend gave Luigi the jaguar pitch.

"Doesn't this already have a villain in it?" He asked Luigi. "Starvation due to lack of agility. How is that not a 'bad guy?' In fact, the jaguar image can be threaded throughout the entire presentation. It represents the core of the problem and has lots of emotional content. It also allows the manager, or board of directors, to identify with the problem and its solution. It allows them to think their company is like a jaguar: They want to follow the market closely and be versatile enough to take full advantage of last-minute conditions."

Luigi looked confused, so our hero tried to drive the point home again.

"It's all about rapid response!"

Luigi laughed.

"You'll find that sometimes you'll develop a story, only to have the meaning lost on someone else. There's another technique that you're going to learn on your journey that will help you bring your opening and the images you use more in line with your specific product. You've already packed a lot of good stuff in your presentation that clearly shows your audience how using your product will benefit them. But you need a real villain – some evil or undesirable thing that poses a real risk to your audience's situation. Try something like..."

He thought for a moment, then continued.

"Instill a connection. The jaguar starved because he wasn't agile enough, yes. But then you need to add something like, 'With our product, that cannot happen. Leading companies use our product because it allows them to react quickly enough to deal with last-minute market changes.'"

"Wow! I actually like that! I surprise myself sometimes!" the Italian said, getting excited.

Our friend clapped his hands.

"That's really impressive. I've been learning such great things over the past few days. I am so grateful to you, your wife, and everyone else."

Luigi smiled.

"You're welcome, but don't think the work is over yet. You will pay the price soon enough."

Again with that threat. Our hero felt uneasy every time he heard that phrase. He wondered how much it was going to ultimately cost him to know the best selling method in the world.

He was thinking this was probably in the five-thousand-dollar ballpark. Maybe that was the right price. Depending on what else was coming in the next steps. Yeah, he would offer 5 grand and hoped the StorySculptor would be satisfied.

Luigi noticed that he was worried."Well," he said, "there is no free lunch."

Our friend looked at him with a sad face, and the Italian burst out in laughing."Don't worry; it won't be too expensive. Let's focus on breakfast now. Your coffee must be totally cold!"

Training Day

Last night, our hero had had an abysmal failure. He'd tried his "strong opening" with a woman. He cringed as he replayed the scene in his mind.

"Wow, I'll bet your dad was a terrorist," had been his opening line. The woman had turned around with an irritated expression.

"What?"

"Must be. Because you look so bombastic."

The woman rolled her eyes, turned around, and walked away, leaving him standing there feeling like a complete idiot. Fortunately, nobody around them seemed to notice his spectacular failure. He allowed himself a single moment of self-pity. *I didn't even make that up!* His inner voice whined. I got it from a song! *So what gives?!*

Even in the midst of his embarrassment, he had been grateful that he hadn't tried to use that opener with the beautiful redhead at the coffee shop. He told himself that the other woman was just a test subject. Besides, he had been drinking, so he wasn't on top of his game. He wondered, however, if he would be brave enough to approach the redhead without a little "liquid courage" in his veins.

Our hero pondered these things from his favorite seat at his favorite coffee shop. He sipped his latte and kept watch for the redhead. He thought about opening lines. Terrorists were too aggressive, so they were out. From Luigi Lombardi, he had learned that the villain didn't always need to be a person.

For example, the wolf in Little Red Riding Hood is a great villain, he told himself. Why was he suddenly thinking about fairy tales? No matter. The witch in Snow White was another memorable antagonist. There were villains everywhere in such tales. He didn't know why his mind kept going back to fairy tales.

I can't remember any of the technical specs of the first products I ever sold, but I remember these fairy tales from grade school!

He was definitely starting to understand the sticking power of stories and becoming a disciple for why storytelling was the best sales strategy of all time.

Good stories have staying power. They can stick around for months or even years. This made stories the best sales tools in the world.

After two hours of waiting for the redhead, our hero decided to get on with his day, thoughts of villains still dancing in his head. Maybe my villain is loneliness, He thought to himself, making a mental note to think about it some more after his first appointment. In the meantime, it was time to face an entirely different species of villain: his boss. He had to go to his office where he had an appointment with his predator.

Good luck with that, he thought.

7 Vaccinated

It took him a week to get there. His boss had signed him up for a trade show and sent him off across the world. His job was to fly over, make a presentation, attend other conference sessions, and develop a new customer base. It had been quite a tall order, but our hero was happy to report he had successfully made sales and acquired new customers. Even so, he had hoped to achieve more. According to his boss, this was the premier trade fair of the year. The Big Show, so to say. This was the venue to boost his figures, according to his boss, and our hero had therefore spent a great amount of time and energy preparing. Unfortunately, now he had to go back to his boss with the fact that customers were flocking to the internet in increasing numbers and ordering online. Many had even shifted to online networking, preferring to save themselves the trade fair expenses in favor of getting pitched to over the web.

This may have been the premier trade fair some years ago, but now it was, well, just another run-of-the-mill event. Needless to say, he was not satisfied at all.

Despite the poor fair attendance, he had used the opportunity to hone the StorySculptor's sales method (the best in the world!), which was already beginning to awaken a certain hope within our friend. The crowds may have been thin and the visitors cautious, but he had landed some big fish. The "jaguar technique," as he'd taken to calling it, was really working. When he called out to people walking by his booth, they were amazed to learn about the jaguar and how our friend's product could give them similar agility. Without his jaguar technique, the show would have been a huge disappointment. He was happy that he had been able to leverage the StorySculptor team's advice already. He was confident he would become a StorySculptor himself very soon.

Now he was on his way to his next appointment. As expected, Luigi had given him the name and phone number of the next link in the StorySculptor's chain. He had the yellow sticky note in his pocket. *Sarah Cooper*, it read. Our friend was already intrigued by the meeting, as Luigi had whispered that this Sarah Cooper was "greater than the giant," whatever that meant. If that was any reference to Kim Labonte, she would be very tall, indeed. Apparently she was a driving instructor.

With only an hour to kill, our friend dropped in to his favorite coffee shop and ordered a latte macchiato. He searched for the redhead as he waited for his drink, but she wasn't there. He grabbed the latte in a "to go" cup and sipped it as he made his way to the driving school.

Standing in front of the address Luigi had scrawled down for him, our hero wasn't sure that he had the right place. There was a large bus parked in front of the building, emblazoned with an advertisement for the school. It read, "Around the World with Sarah." There was a large truck parked next to the bus, and its trailer was covered with a shiny tarpaulin that bore the image of an airplane and the words, "Sarah Makes Your World Go 'Round." Very funny, wasn't it?

He entered the building, which appeared to be a storefront with a large bay window. Inside, however, it seemed more like a classroom than a store. There was a large desk off to one side; the woman sitting there was short and slim with black hair and dark eyes. *Surely this couldn't be the Sarah, he thought...could it?* He found it strange to believe, but he sensed a certain air of authority emanating from her. It was as if she was a navy SEAL or some other elite force commander.

This feeling seemed confirmed as he approached the desk and saw that she was wearing military fatigues. The woman rose and smiled. She moved peacefully, deliberately, and with controlled power. She shook his hand. "Welcome! Thanks for coming in today. It's nice to meet you."

"Oh yes, thank you for making time to meet with me."

"I know that you're on a journey, the trip arranged by the StorySculptor. And I can see in your eyes that you're full of questions, like whether someone as small as me can actually drive buses and trucks." Her eyes sparkled. "Let me assure you, I can."

"Well...yeah, but I'm more confused because Luigi described you as 'bigger than the giant.'"

"The giant?"

Our hero regaled her with his list of nicknames and asked if he could add her to that list as 'the driving instructor.' She nodded and gestured to a leather sofa in the lounge area.

"Why don't we have a seat, and I'll try to answer your questions. Coffee?"

Despite already having a latte that morning, our hero accepted a cup of black coffee, thinking it would at least give him something to do with his hands.

"So! Let's start with the 'larger than the giant' notion. What did you expect? A woman taller than Kim Labonte?" She chuckled and took a sip from the steaming mug. "That would be quite the spectacle. I'd be more of a monster than your friend who sells haunted houses."

"Absolutely. I'm glad reality disproved my expectations." He was pleased with his quick save.

"It's always a question of expectations, isn't it? Do you think that, in addition to trucks and buses, I could pilot a tank?"

"No doubt about it."

"Aha! Now you've allowed yourself to be misled again! As you can see, I am clearly not bigger than the giant, and I don't know the first thing about piloting tanks. You've been tricked!"

Hey, that's unfair, he thought, feeling embarrassed and mildly annoyed with Luigi.

"Why would Luigi say those things, then?"

Sarah just laughed.

"Who said anything about Luigi? You tricked yourself. I never told you that I could drive a tank nor did Luigi. Your brain whispered it to you, and you made an assumption. Our brains are such wondrous and mysterious things, aren't they?"

She paused.

"One more question. At what color of traffic light should you stop?"

Red, of course. But now he felt uncertain. Was this another trick? He didn't want to fall headlong into another trap, so he didn't answer at all.

Sarah burst out laughing.

"Ha! You've just demonstrated my point. You were so scared of falling into another trap that you got confused by a simple question and remained silent."

He didn't like this.

Sarah raised a hand in a conciliatory gesture.

"I apologize for this nasty game. I just wanted to show you how often we are guided by assumptions and irrelevant external circumstances. When that happens, we lose control of our brains and switch to autopilot. Sometimes that's good, but often it isn't." *Duh*, thought our hero. "I suppose this is another method for Storytelling," he speculated.

"And how," answered the little woman. "If we create an environment that causes customers to think in a certain way before we even say anything, then we have a huge step up on them. Why are you wearing a suit?"

"Because I sell to large companies and the executives, so I can't get away with jeans and sneakers."

"Precisely!" she exclaimed, nearly spilling her coffee. "You want to make a good first impression. We follow these social conventions to direct the minds of our customers to our advantage."

"Doesn't that contradict the strong opening, though?" our hero asked.

"Not at all. The strong opening comes *after* the first impression. We direct the customer's brain to where we want it to go, and then we take control with the strong opening."

Strong words.

"Look, I've done it to you already. First, I made you assume that I could pilot a tank, and then I unsettled you with the traffic light question. It worked, didn't it?"

Our hero had to agree.

"Today, I'll explain two elements that will help you control your sale. You'll use these techniques to slip your story into your customer's subconscious, get it stuck there, and leave your customer feeling enthusiastic about your product. Even better, these techniques sell your product to the customer over and over again, which probably sounds like overkill but is actually a tremendous help."

"Why do you think I wear a military uniform instead of a business suit?" Sarah asked.

"I was wondering the same thing, especially since you can't drive tanks." They both laughed.

"Seriously, though," our hero continued, "I'll bet no man would ever believe that a petite woman in a business suit could teach him how to drive trucks and buses. He probably wouldn't even get in the cab if she was driving it." Sarah nodded enthusiastically.

"Exactly. But everything changes when I'm in my uniform. When I wear this, nobody doubts for a second that I could drive tanks or kill you thirty different ways using only a folded cocktail napkin." She chuckled. "Truth is, I could only do it in seventeen ways."

She drained her mug and set it down on the coffee table.

"I'm always doing experiments here at my school. I'll ask a student, 'How much fuel does it take to bring a cruise ship across the Atlantic? Does it take more or less than 100,000 gallons?' Some say less, some say more. Nobody ever agrees. Then I'll ask another group the same question, but I'll ask if it takes more or less than 500,000 gallons to cross the ocean. Do you know what happens then? The guesses skyrocket. The average guess in the second group is *five times higher* than the average of the first group. And neither group realizes that they have been manipulated."

"Yeah, unfortunately I'm all too familiar with that. A while ago I was watching the Home Shopping Network, and I saw this amazing set of knives for a great price. The best part was right at the end of the advertisement: 'This set can be yours for...not $500, not $400, not even $300, but it can be yours for the low price of just $189.' So I bought it, of course, and the knives were terrific. Then I saw the exact same set the next week at the mall for only $90."

"That's one of the oldest tricks in the book," Sarah agreed. "I know a salesman from a bus company who invites customers into his office and serves them champagne. He tells them, 'I just sold a dozen luxury liners! I'm so happy I thought maybe you'd like to celebrate with me. Our luxury liners are very popular, providing our tour operators with real value and tremendously improving bookings. They cost almost $300,000, but it's money well spent. You know what? That salesman sells 20 percent more in total sales volume than his colleagues do.'"

"Like the knife set trick on steroids," our hero said, grinning.

"Exactly! This is a technique called priming. Your story contains a prime, an element designed to shape your customers' thinking. This provides you with the power to define the framework within which your customers will operate."

Our hero had experienced this firsthand and knew how effective the technique was. He felt a flood of gratitude. It was so simple and efficient! He wanted to thank Sarah profusely, but she wasn't yet finished.

"That isn't all," she continued. "A related technique is called anchoring the prime. Think about the traffic light again. The correct answer, of course, is 'red.' When we see a red light, we slow down. It doesn't matter if you're driving in the US or somewhere else. Similarly, in most countries a red octagon provokes a stopping response. Our brains go on autopilot. You could be completely distracted, but if you see a red light or a red octagonal sign, you'll stop. Once you pull into your driveway you might not remember all the turns you made to get home, but you know you stopped at the red lights."

"Yeah, otherwise I wouldn't have made it home in once piece," our hero added.

"Exactly! So, the red light and the stop sign are anchors, meaning that our reaction to them is anchored so deeply within us that it becomes automatic. This is one of the most powerful psychological tools a salesperson can use!"

Sarah made it all sound so thrilling. Anchors. Our hero thought back to his days in school, when he'd learned about the scientist Ivan Pavlov and his famous dogs. Pavlov trained his dogs to associate a bell with food. Eventually, the dogs would automatically salivate when they heard the bell, even if they did not receive any food.

"This is a conditioned response, like with Pavlov's dogs."

"Exactly. And just as Pavlov trained his dogs, we can train our customers. Sounds bad, but it's true."

Wow! Customers can be trained, he thought.

"So we're going to make them drool?" he asked with a mischievous twinkle in his eye.

"Such a smartass," she grinned. "Another example is couples who have a 'song.' It's the same story every time: 'Ooh, this is our song! This is when I kissed her for the first time.' For them, the song is an anchor."

"Could a logo be an anchor?" inquired our hero.

"Sure. Everything that evokes an automatic feeling or emotion is an anchor. You think about sports the minute you see the Nike Swoosh, right? Maybe it reminds us to exercise more or causes us to think about the time when we ran in the New York Marathon because we did it in Nike sneakers. Songs can also remind us of products, which is why jingles and theme songs are so important. Play the music and make a sale. Show the picture and make another sale! You see? Brands are anchors."

"What about trademarks?"

"Trademarks are anchors too, even if they only trigger feelings rather than the urge to buy a specific product. Trademarks form our expectations and conjure up mental images. Every parent of a teenager fights the battle of the brands. If your jeans aren't made by whatever the trendy brand is at the moment, you're unbearably uncool."

Our hero had another question.

"So, that would mean that the nicknames I've given to the StorySculptor and his friends, those are anchors too, correct? Even if I don't remember their real names instantly, I remember what they've taught me."

"Absolutely," replied Sarah. "These are very powerful tools, but BE CAREFUL! It's important to understand that the brain doesn't filter." She raised her voice and pointed her index finger at his chest. "Once the impulse is anchored, the autopilot reaction becomes automatic, even if you've triggered a negative impulse! This can ruin a sale!"

Our friend leaned forward, not wanting to miss a word.

"The extreme example is post-traumatic stress syndrome, where a word or a smell or a snippet of a song can instantly take someone back to some horrible event. Even in milder cases, triggering the wrong anchor can make someone cry or get depressed, which isn't exactly conducive to making sales."

"Is it also possible to trigger an anchor unintentionally?" he asked.

"Yes, unfortunately. That's why there's always a danger in using well-known, omnipresent anchors, like an athlete, a song, a movie title, colors. They're known to almost everyone already, yet the emotions a certain athlete triggers can be very different depending on who you are and where you come from. Regional differences can often result in unintentionally triggered anchors. This happens a lot with colors."

"Oh, I get it now!" Our hero was elated.

"I can't wait to try this! If I'm hearing you correctly, I should prime them, identify the correct anchor, and use this to establish communication and rapport with my clients before I get them into 'buying mode.'"

"Exactly," said Sarah. "We call it 'firing the anchor.' When you fire your anchor, it evokes positive associations and emotions in your client which are then transferred to you and your product."

Our hero had just relearned a very important lesson and felt the strong compulsion to leave before he became overwhelmed with any other information. He thanked her for her time, and she gave the obligatory hint about "paying the price" before seeing him out.

When he reached the door, he turned around one last time, saying, "One thing I now know for sure: Whenever I see a woman in camouflage I'll think of you. You're that deeply anchored in me now."

Sarah laughed and waved good-bye.

A simulated cough

Our hero sat in his favorite coffee shop, deep in thought. He hadn't slept well, and kept having nightmares about anchors. They were everywhere! He was being chased by anchors, and ships shot their anchors at him like giant bullets.

He was still fascinated by the idea of using these anchors to reconnect with the prospective clients he met in Chicago and was hoping for an opportunity to test his skills.

Wasn't the simple line, "Hi we met at the fair in Chicago" some sort of anchor?

"Excuse me?" came a voice from the left.

Our hero's head snapped up, and he realized that he had been talking quietly to himself. He turned in the direction of the voice and almost fell off his stool. It was her! How did she sidle up next to him without him noticing?

The redhead obviously thought that he had been mumbling to her. Nice, he thought to himself. Our hero cleared his throat to buy a few seconds in which to formulate a response. He couldn't use his normal "jaguar" opening because he already had her attention. He felt his panic level rising rapidly, so he coughed again. That gave him just enough time to come up with his pitch.

Yes, it was essentially a pitch, wasn't it?

He tried to remind himself that this was just like any other sales situation, only he needed to sell himself rather than a piece of technology.

He refused to let himself consider whether or not he would have a second chance with her. Such thoughts were counterproductive and distracting, and our hero had learned enough by this point to know his best chance at winning her over was through storytelling. He said,

"Hi. I was thinking about jaguars. Not the cars – the animal."

She raised an eyebrow. He continued:

"Do you know why jaguars survive?"

She pursed her lips.

"Because jaguars are very fast and skilled hunters?" He liked her melodious voice and was thrilled that she'd actually answered him.

"Because he can slow down when he needs to."

"Interesting," she replied, "I've never seen one, but I guess it's obvious. If the prey attempts to elude the jaguar by cutting back and forth as it runs, the jaguar will starve unless he can do the same."

Beauty and brains. Nice, he thought.

"Do you study biology?" she asked.

"No, I'm learning a new sales technique."

"I didn't know that was a major."

"No, I'm already in sales; my formal studies are behind me. Recently I've been having problems with my numbers, but thankfully the StorySculptor is helping me learn how to increase my sales volume through storytelling."

He gulped his latte.

"Are you in college?" he ventured.

"Yeah. I'm studying psychology."

"Really? You would love the stuff I'm learning from this guy called the StorySculptor. It's all applied psychology, presented in terms laypeople can understand and use." She nodded and smiled.

"That does sound interesting. Unfortunately, I'm running a bit late for my next lecture, and it isn't one I can afford to miss. But I really would like to learn more about jaguars. Do you come here often? I think I may have seen you here before."

His heart was beating faster and faster. She remembered him! He forced himself to stay calm while arranging a follow-up date, but it was hard to remain calm until he had "landed the deal," so to say. She'd laid the groundwork. Only a total fool could screw it up now!

"Yes, this is my favorite coffee shop," he said. *Ever since I saw you here*, he thought to himself.

8 Exciting times

It was Saturday, and our hero was excited because he was supposed to meet the StorySculptor again that day, not to mention that he'd scored a date with the gorgeous redhead! He had arranged to have breakfast with her on Monday, as she was visiting her parents over the weekend and wouldn't be back till Monday.

This was an exciting time for him, personally and professionally. Over the course of the last few days, he'd laughed, he'd been scared, he'd learned, he'd fumed, he'd enjoyed himself, and experienced a panoply of other emotions, too. Since rebuilding his sales presentation he'd landed two new contracts that he knew would never have responded favorably to his old style. He had confidence that his sales would continue to increase as he gained experience and polish. He was very much looking forward to demonstrating his progress to the StorySculptor and felt ready to pass any test the StorySculptor might throw his way.

From Dr. Susan Lombardi, he'd learned about the human brain and its hemispheres. To maximize sales, he knew that he needed to circumvent the analytical, fact-loving left brain in favor of the emotional right brain, which responded best to stories. Selling stories meant selling products. Next, he'd visited Kim Labonte and learned the importance of knowing one's outcome frame. He now knew that if he didn't have his destination in view, the journey would be pointless. In sales, this meant defining the outcome frame before deciding on a pitch strategy. It makes a big difference whether you're trying to sell to a scientist or to a manager, but different presentations for different types of people will make for a singular outcome: success. Procurement managers are interested in numbers; scientists are interested in numbers too, but different numbers. The important thing is to know which numbers will excite and be internalized by which person.

Next came the visit to Mr. Monster, Tom Schneider. He still had vivid memories of the creepy, darkened hallway and the costumed horrors that greeted him on his way into Schneider's office. That in itself proved how effective the storytelling method was, and how Schneider's "strong opening" was an essential component of it. He could hear Schneider telling him, *Use something surprising, something exciting, something witty to captivate your customers and cancel out any ambient noise. Astonish them and arouse their curiosity so you have their undivided attention.*

After Mr. Monster came the Italiano Luigi Lombardi, the raven-haired racecar driver married to Dr. Susan Lombardi. Luigi emphasized the need for a villain in every story, even in sales presentations. Of course, he was quick to point out that a villain doesn't have to be a fearsome monster; it is often just an idea or an image. Without the villain, clients have no benchmark to judge the value of the products or services being sold. He thought about Hollywood. Each and every blockbuster had a villain. Batman had the Joker, Bond had Dr. No; there was no way a movie would become a blockbuster without a villain, and his sales wouldn't reach blockbuster level without one either.

He turned his thoughts to Sarah, the military-fatigued driving instructor. She was a truly special person, and our hero admired the way that she had deftly carved out a niche for herself in the male-dominated world of truck and bus driving. Sarah taught him about perception, deception, and assumptions. Using her *priming* technique, she was able to direct a person's mind where she wanted it to go, knowing that the brain was properly aligned to receive her message. Priming feeds the brain framing information that allows the salesperson to determine the parameters for the sales pitch. Consider a potential customer with a hard budget of $10,000. That customer is apt to try and negotiate a lower rate to avoid spending all of that money. The salesperson can solve this problem before it appears by priming the customer, telling him or her that the company has just completed a million-dollar job. Suddenly, the customer worries if his $10,000 job will be too small or insignificant for the company to care about, and feels fortunate to "win" a spot on the company's order list. An effective salesperson always uses priming, even if it's only a simple statement telling the customer they will be thrilled with the amazing offer they are about to get (which has, unbeknownst to the customer, also been offered to every other potential client).

Sarah, the spitfire in battle gear, hadn't just introduced our hero to priming, she'd also demonstrated *anchoring*, another invaluable technique to be used. Setting proper anchors that are conducive to the sales goal encourages the potential customer's brain to go on autopilot and produce a predictable response. When a driver sees a red light (which is an anchor, evoking the desire to stop), he automatically brakes. Jingles, logos, and slogans are excellent examples of anchoring as well. A wise salesperson takes advantage of anchors to elicit pleasant feelings in customers, or to help the customer to recall a previously discussed product or service. On follow-up calls, the salesperson fires those anchors, trusting they will evoke a strong, clear, and positive recollection of a previous conversation or unique product features.

This technique is remarkably effective, but requires caution, too. Anchors also have the potential to evoke extremely negative emotions based on past experiences or cultural codes the salesperson can't control. Wise salespeople try to avoid triggering unpleasant reactions by avoiding popular and controversial anchors.

Our hero had understood and practiced all of these techniques, nut he also was very cautious with them, as he knew he hadn't mastered them yet. Before and after each sales pitch, he reviewed his paperwork, making sure that he was prepared and had hit on every necessary step. At first, there was so much to remember that he felt intimidated, almost like he was drowning in a sea of information. With practice, however, those feelings slowly began to disappear.

Reviewing his paperwork gave our hero valuable opportunities to learn about his strengths and weaknesses and about what worked in specific situations. He began by working on priming, then on strong openings and anchors. He worked his way down the list of skills he'd learned, mastering one before moving on to the next. Before long, it seemed like second nature to incorporate all of the steps in every sales pitch.

He was also spending more time studying the sales material of his competitors, and more than once a smile spread over his face as he discovered that they had missed the most important part of a good sales pitch: a good story. Most of them didn't have a villain. They didn't use anchors outside their corporate logos or slogans. Granted, he hadn't either until a few weeks ago, but what a difference a few weeks can make. He almost felt sorry for his competitors at times. Never mind, he was at war, and he would take no prisoners!

Our hero had made sales. That much was certain. But how reliable were these numbers? Could he count on his "luck" continuing? Was it all just a big craps shoot?

Selling just felt so much easier when it was accompanied by a story that penetrated the mind and emotions of potential customers. Stories that inspire are the most memorable; they're also the easiest for the salesperson to remember and tell.

A good story sticks with the customer. A good story excites the customer. A good story gets retold and makes the customer an avid fan, spurring them to promote the product and act as a brand advocate at no added cost to the company. A good story was like magic, that was for sure.

It felt great, so great that our hero was almost looking forward to his meeting with the StorySculptor, having forgotten that he still had a price to pay and that loomed over his head.

9 A Barbecue Party

There was a parking space right in front of the house. Alright! The StorySculptor lived in a residential area where street parking was scarce. Consequently, our hero had left early and given himself plenty of extra time to hunt for a suitable spot. He now found himself 15 minutes ahead of schedule. He decided to stroll around the neighborhood for a few minutes so as not to inconvenience the StorySculptor with an early arrival. He turned a corner and heard someone call his name. It was the StorySculptor, sitting outside in his garden with his laptop open.

“Take the garden entrance,” he said, “You’re right in front of the door.”

Our hero approached the StorySculptor and shook his hand.

“Welcome,” the StorySculptor said, “Have a seat! I’m very happy to see you again.” He gestured to the adjacent chair, inviting our friend to join him.

“So, young man, how have you been? Have you learned anything? I hope that you weren’t disappointed.”

“Disappointed? How could I be disappointed after everything you have given me?” said our friend, “Thanks to you and your friends, I now know the best sales method on Earth! I learned so many important things and had fun all along the way. The whole experience has left me feeling nothing short of elated.”

The StorySculptor laughed. “I’ve heard nothing but good things about your visits. Susan said she caught you off guard with her physics lecture.”

"Yep, she did a find job of confusing the heck out of me, the monster scared the living daylights out of me, and I must admit to being both surprised and impressed by the driving instructor."

"Monster? Driving instructor?" the StorySculptor look confused.

"Yeah, I actually gave nicknames to each person along the way to help me remember what they taught me," our friend explained.

The Professor

Susan Lombardi - impressed upon me the importance of appealing to the target's right brain, which is best done with stories.

The Giant

Kim Labonte showed me how important it is to establish your goals before trying to sell anything.

The Monster

Tom Schneider, scared me out of my wits the minute I walked into his building. He wanted to give me the same experience all of his first-time customers get. This taught me volumes about the necessity of a strong opening to any sales pitch.

The Italiano

is, of course, Luigi Lombardi. I'll never forget that guy! He showed me how villains are an essential part of any memorable story and therefore any effective sales pitch. I learned that the villain doesn't always have to be a monster or something supernatural; it could be an event or a consequence as well.

The driving instructor

Sarah, taught me about priming and anchoring. She demonstrated that we can frame the thinking of our customers without them knowing it, then we can take advantage of anchors to elicit automatic responses. It's like putting the sales decision on autopilot.

“I’m curious,” said the StorySculptor, “What nickname have you given me?”

"I didn’t. You are the StorySculptor."

"Oh, well, it’s an honor. Thank you." He was visibly pleased. "To get the most out of what you’ve learned thus far, you need to learn three additional techniques.”

Three other techniques. Very cool.

The StorySculptor’s wife popped in and offered beverages. The StorySculptor made the necessary introductions:

"Honey, this is the young man I told you about. I sent him on a journey to learn the best sales method in the world, and he’s come back from his fifth stop to report back on his progress. Before long he’ll be a master storyteller in his own right.”

"Yes," his wife said to our hero, "That he may.” She gestured toward her husband. “After all, you’re learning from the best in the business.” She smiled and disappeared, soon returning with a fresh pot of coffee.

"Anyone can learn these techniques,” said the StorySculptor. "It isn’t rocket science, after all. Nevertheless, it is very important that we give the customer what he really wants."

"Of course. That’s why we need outcome frames," said our hero.

"What about a customer who wants to buy a station wagon?" asked the StorySculptor.

Here comes the test, our hero thought.

"Well, that customer needs to transport people or items on a regular basis. The customer probably has a large family or enjoys equipment-intensive sports. Or maybe he's in a band and needs to haul around speakers and a drum kit."

"All true," said the StorySculptor, "but those are general statements applicable to all station wagons. We are in technical sales: sales by data, facts, and figures. How would our customer decide which model to buy? Let's say he can choose from three brands and they have identical performance statistics. What does this customer really want in his heart of hearts?"

The customer wants a combination of everything you just said, thought our friend, but still wasn't sure, so he remained silent.

"You can't imagine, right?" asked the StorySculptor. He leaned forward conspiratorially and whispered, "He wants to feel good after the purchase!"

The StorySculptor turned his computer monitor around so our friend could see it. He showed him a slide.

People don't care about our product; they only care about themselves!

"This is the brutal reality. This is the core of the whole. Of course, we think that is not true of ourselves. That's not to say that we don't care about others, and their welfare isn't important to us. We are social beings, but when we're making a purchase, that's not entirely true.

People only make a purchase when they are excited about it. That, and once some important questions have been answered.

He pressed the mouse and another slide appeared:

What's in it for me?

"That, my friend, is the crucial question. This is the question the customer will always ask themselves. Always unconsciously, of course, unless the salesperson starts to get on their nerves, then they will most likely ask it directly to your face. That is the question we always need to answer."

Our hero sat back to think about what the StorySculptor was saying. He knew it was true. What was that unknown, undefined quality that could ruin an otherwise perfect sale? He was frequently frustrated by clients who seemed pleased and promised to call, but wound up disappearing. Upon further inquiry, these customers usually answered in a friendly manner that they are in the middle of a important project which needed to be finished before they could consider anything else. Either that or they made some excuse about budget problems or the like. There was never a clear "no," but never a clear "yes" either. Frustrating. He always felt totally powerless. At times he wished they would just tell him "no" so he could move on and concentrate on other things rather than stall endlessly and fruitlessly.

Turning to the StorySculptor, he said, "Is that the reason why customers do not order even though they like the product?"

"Yes, but it isn't the only reason." He advanced to the next slide:

Am I putting myself on the line?

At what risk to me?

“This is a very, very important question for most people. Your sales target might get fired if he makes a bad purchasing decision. Often, sales are lost because of this fear alone. Many buying agents would prefer to remain with an inferior product rather than face the possibility of managerial wrath by switching.”

Our hero nodded emphatically. “Wow, now I understand why some sales drag along forever and never seems to close, despite having a great rapport with the potential customer.”

The StorySculptor agreed and continued:

“Nobody makes decisions in a vacuum. This is true in and out of the office. People are surrounded by other people: friends, family, neighbors, colleagues, etc. They want to be respected and admired, not ridiculed. It’s human nature to avoid things that may result in getting us laughed at or made fun of. These are the basic ideas that we need to consider when we develop a story. Note that you must always consider both of these questions."

The StorySculptor clicked to the next slide.

How will I feel after the purchase?

Will people think I’m a fool when they see what I’ve bought?

"This is where the importance of the well-craft story comes in. A story that inspires and entertains. These stories should stick in the minds of our customers to the point that they can't help but think about and talk about them repeatedly, spreading the word to family members, friends, and colleagues."

"That makes sense." Our hero smiled. "I distinctly remember the time my uncle bought my mother a brand new blender. My father had no respect for domesticity and looked down upon people who got excited about things like new appliances. Anyway, one day the whole neighborhood was having a cookout, so my uncle took the opportunity to bring the new blender over.

"My father took the opportunity right away to make fun of my uncle. 'Well, you always did like the women's work. I'm glad somebody is taking care of our kitchen appliances now because I have to do the man's work, like cooking the steaks.'" Our hero laughed. "A very embarrassing situation for my uncle, but he was well prepared and laughed back, 'I know, but you really shouldn't underestimate the power of a blender. You're not going to believe what this thing can do. Check it out.'

That being said, he whipped out his iPad and showed a clip of the same model blender pulverizing a real iPhone. It was incredible. Suddenly everyone who had been laughing at my uncle for his silly 'feminine' kitchen appliances was speechless, including my dad.

"Well done," the StorySculptor chuckled appreciatively. "How did that go on?"

“Well, my dad is a strong man, so he took it in stride. ‘Touche,’ he had said and then proceeded to blend every type of food possible with the new power blender, including what seemed like bucket upon bucket of ice for his margaritas!”

“Awesome, I wish I had been part of it. A great story and a very good anchor for you,” the StorySculptor continued. “This is an excellent example of how important it is to answer the questions What’s in it for me? and Will people think I am a fool later?

“Right. That’s a really good point. I’m always trying to think about how the upper-level management will react to my products. It seems the most successful stories I create are those that I feel my potential customer will easily be able to repeat to his managers when justifying the purchase,” our hero reflected.

"And now for something completely new!" said the StorySculptor, stretching his arms theatrically. “Here comes the grand finale!”

“Something new? Are there really still more tools for improving my storytelling?” asked our friend. “If I learn this one last technique, will I have finally mastered the art of selling?”

The StorySculptor leaned back and crossed his arms over his chest. He had a pensive expression on his face.

"Riddle me this: What do you think is the biggest mistake a salesperson can make after a seemingly perfect presentation which has clearly excited the customer?"

Our hero shook his head.

"I see this all the time and it takes every ounce of my self control to not jump in and save them from their error, even with the best storytellers in the business. When I see it, I can't believe it, but then it happens again in the next sales pitch and looks like there is nothing that can stop it. Do you have any idea what it could be?"

"Is the mistake that they end the meeting prematurely?" Our friend was drawing from personal experience. Many times, after a splendid presentation with a captivated audience, he had the impulse to end the meeting immediately, fearing he might break the mood and damage the deal. Some of his colleagues routinely took the opposite approach, gabbing and talking in circles long after the customer was convinced. He felt that this was equally unwise.

The StorySculptor nodded. "All of these storytelling techniques come to nothing if the salesperson doesn't know when to stop talking. It's like baking a beautiful cake and then dropping it on the way into the dining room. You need to create your masterpiece, then you need to be silent and enjoy the cake. Is that so complicated?"

Our friend felt the tension in the StorySculptor's voice. This really got to him.

"You simply need to anchor the strongest argument, complete the story, and then stop talking. This is absolutely critical!" the StorySculptor finished.

Just like that kids' game where the first person to speak loses, thought our hero.

The StorySculptor had fallen into silence. Our hero waited... 45 seconds. He continued to wait...Three minutes. He didn't know what to do. Was it rude to sit there in silence? Should he say something? He cleared his throat.

"So what do I do if nobody says anything for a long time?"

The StorySculptor broke into a broad smile.

"Just like what's happening right now? How long do you think we've been sitting here in silence?"

"At least eight to ten minutes," said our hero with conviction.

The StorySculptor laughed and consulted his iPhone.

"My dear friend, I timed it here on my app. Only 53 seconds have gone by!"

Our friend's jaw dropped. The StorySculptor continued:

"Yes, and these situations are uncomfortable for everyone involved, not just the salesperson. If your client isn't an experienced sales professional, he'll eventually say something. Ideally, this is when the customer agrees to buy something, but this can only happen if the seller makes strong enough statements and then shuts his mouth."

He showed our hero another slide:

The one who speaks first loses!

"So you're saying that a strong closing is just as important as a strong opening?"

"Basically," replied the StorySculptor. "When we make a strong opening, we garner the client's undivided attention. Then we tell our tale, anchoring its strongest element. Then we fire that anchor and ask for a conclusion. We ask the customer to buy!"

He emphasized the last words a second time. *"We ask for the signature!"*

The StorySculptor continued: "This is where many salespeople fail. They're afraid because they don't know how to respond if the customer says no, and they're afraid that their magical fairy tale will be dashed by that one little word. The root of the problem is that these salespeople don't truly believe that they are helping their customers and that what they are offering is the best solution. These are the salespeople who would rather adjourn a meeting than take a risk by asking the customer to buy. Remember that salespeople are people too! Customers ask themselves what negative consequences they may face as a result of the purchase, but salespeople also ask themselves, 'What do I have to lose? How risky is this for me?'"

Our hero was flabbergasted. Yet again, the StorySculptor was right on the money. He knew many colleagues that submitted pitch reports saying, Customers were very impressed. Good pitch. Next appointment scheduled in four weeks' time. This was a common tactic salespeople used to keep their sales report clean. Customers who agreed to a future meeting could not yet be classified as a failed sale, thereby allowing the salesperson to avoid any blemishes on their record. When these sellers did finally make a sale, then their record appears, superficially, to be only successes. Of course, the reality is that their sales aren't consistent.

He shared his thoughts with the StorySculptor, who immediately agreed with him.

"Precisely, but here's the catch: If you have developed a good story and convey this well, then you've got yourself the perfect sales pitch, and you've wowed your customers with it. Why then risk ruining that with such a blunt question?"

Our hero thought. He found no reason why a seller under these circumstances should change his modus operandi.

The StorySculptor interrupted his thoughts and answered the question for him:

"The solution is the story itself. You must inspire your clients, get them excited when they think about your products, and ensure they understand why they should pick your products instead of the competition's. This means that they have to understand what negative consequences they risk if they choose poorly. Ultimately, you need to help the client understand that the dangers of not buying are greater than the danger of their boss's wrath. If you can manage all of that, you have a real home run!" The StorySculptor was fully engaged now and spoke with a tremendous level of energy.

“Wow!” our friend was excited now, too. It all made so much sense. He felt like the true secret of selling had just been revealed to him, but then some doubts crept in.

“But not every story turns out so incredibly well.”

"True," said the StorySculptor. "Developing a perfect story is easy with the techniques you have learned on your journey, but of course there is no guarantee that it will work on the first run. It will surely need some adjustments and will get better and better over time, but that’s why I’m emphasizing the strong conclusion. Anchor your strongest argument and call upon it during your conclusion. Then...” he made a portentous gesture and lowered his voice. He was silent. Our hero smiled at him. He was silent too. 30 seconds passed, then 45 seconds and finally it was over a minute.

Our hero understood. He had only to think of his colleague Jim, who was infamous for battering customers with gushing words until they were bored and disengaged. Often, customers signed contracts with Jim simply to shut him up and get him out the door. Interestingly, the sales manager frequently praised Jim’s gift of gab. As the new guy in the company, our hero had shadowed Jim for several days and witnessed first-hand the devastating effects of his motor mouth. The customers always seemed to like Jim on a personal level, but he often lost sales because he didn’t let the customer get a word in edgewise. Eventually, the customers left frustrated.

When our hero mentioned this to Jim, he got rather defensive and cited his top sales record as proof that our hero should keep his opinions to himself. What Jim failed to realize was that client meetings kept getting postponed not because his customers were unprepared, but because he was.

"Well, my young friend," said the StorySculptor. "Now you know the world's best sales method."

Our hero leapt up joyfully and shook the StorySculptor's hand.

“Thank you! Thank you! Thank you!” he exclaimed. The StorySculptor laughed.

“The hardest piece of work is still ahead of you,” he said.

Payday.

Our hero sat down.

“Payday.”

The StorySculptor laughed again. “Yes, but it isn't so bad. Did my colleagues prime you adequately by warning you about payday?”

“You could say that, yeah.”

If he doesn't want money, what is it that he wants? How am I supposed to pay this guy?

"Your journey is just beginning. My team members have years of experience under their belts, so they are even more advanced than you are. You now know how to develop a compelling sales story and understand the psychology behind what you're doing. However..." the StorySculptor raised a hand in apparent warning, as if to say, Stop! Danger ahead!

He adjusted his computer monitor so our hero could read its contents

Knowledge has no power! Applied knowledge has power!

"That means," said the StorySculptor, "that you need to apply these principles every day. You're not a finished product yet. Work with these techniques every day, and your stories will adjust. Watch your customers carefully to see how they react, then take that feedback and adjust your pitch again. What this all means is that you have to..."

He clicked his mouse button.

Practice!

Practice!

And more practice!

The StorySculptor's wife appeared at that point, bearing a tray loaded with colorful fruit juices and tempting snacks. He eagerly shared them with our hero and regaled him with tales from his long and storied career. After some time, the garden gate creaked, and in walked Kim Labonte and Luigi Lombardi. They pulled up chairs of their own and joined the conversation. Over the next several hours, the entire "gang" (as the StorySculptor affectionately referred to them) arrived. The balmy weather couldn't have been better for a cookout, and before long our hero could smell steaks sizzling on the barbecue behind him.

Our hero never wanted the evening to end. Like all good stories, however, this one had a villain. One of the "gang" stood up and asked the StorySculptor,

"So, have you already given him the bill?"

Everyone laughed. Everyone, that is, except our friend, who had been hoping to avoid this part entirely. He forced himself to smile and shifted nervously in his chair. The StorySculptor licked steak sauce off of his fingers and reopened his laptop. Turning the computer so our hero could see, he announced,

"This is the price we expect, if you please..."

Please share our story!

Spread the word across the world!

"Hi Jaguar," she said...

FIN

10 About me

Have you ever mowed a lawn,

landscaped a golf course, or harvested a field of grain? Each of these tasks obviously requires different, specialized tools.

For example, a lawnmower that works on a small domestic yard will be ineffective on a farm. Of course, for a golf course you might even need more than one machine. And this is what I do: not mowing grass, but analyzing what people need to “mow” or “cultivate” and what machine is best for the job. I don’t stop there, either. I also deliver the equipment and train the employees who will be using it to reap the harvest. It sounds fantastic, but there is no stronger analogy. After all, I am the StorySculptor!

Every salesperson works in a target market composed of individuals. I want to stress the idea of individuals here, as I frequently hear people use the phrase “target market” to refer to a hypothetical economic entity independent of it’s people. This is a grave error, but we’re here to talk about my work, not my pet peeves. I analyze markets and determine what products should be sold to which people. This is where I determine what needs to be “cultivated”: a lawn, a golf course, or a farm. I then develop an appropriate sales story that introduces the product or service in question. The story is crafted to enter the customer’s subconscious and live there for a long time. These are the stories that sell!

The next step is training the salespeople to convey this story perfectly, convincingly, and comfortably. They then start to gain new clients and book orders like never before, and their customers come away from the transaction more excited and satisfied, which means they are more likely to talk about it and encouraged their friends, neighbors, and/or colleagues to make the purchase, too.

Am I a sales trainer? A professor? A rhetorician? No! I’m a storyteller. Sales trainers teach selling techniques, rhetoricians know how to persuade with words, and sales consultants are mainly concerned with the structure of the sale and the best methods for controlling distribution. These aren’t optimal sales approaches. Think of it this way: Suppose that you taught your employees how to build a simple lawnmower with a screwdriver, a hammer, and a welding torch. It might take you a while, but eventually you'd have a working lawnmower and your employees would probably be able to build one without your help. Great. Now ask them to build a combine harvester. Can they do it? No! The sad reality is that knowing one skill doesn't mean that you will automatically understand a related one

The stories that I provide are carefully developed, precisely designed, and can be used with great success by any trained salesperson. With them, you and your employees can bring in a bountiful harvest year after year. That is my goal: to give you the perfect strategy to ensure your harvest is plentiful.

From this book, you will learn why it is better to sell via storytelling than by bombarding potential clients with facts and numbers. It will teach you some basic techniques that you need to produce that effective sales story. If you use this approach, you will instantly improve your sales performance. I invite you to explore this storytelling technique, visit my blog for more detailed suggestions, and even get quick tips from me in real time on Twitter. To subscribe to my blog and get notified about new posts, go to www.storysculptor.net .

My Twitter handle is @StorySculptor

I am also happy to help you create the perfect sales story to meet your sales goals. Simply write me an email: jg@storysculptor.net

Storytellers tell stories,

but StorySculptors create them!

A customer once asked me why I'm a StorySculptor. I replied, "Because I develop sales stories." The customer was nonplussed and responded,

"But then you're a storyteller." Then I understood the problem.

Storytellers tell stories, but StorySculptors create them!

You, dear readers, along with your friends, colleagues, or employees are the Storytellers.

You may be thinking, "But I want to learn how to develop stories too!"

Well, here I can help you. I regularly organize and present seminars and workshops in which I offer personalized, hands-on training in story creation. It is not a difficult skill to develop, and anyone can learn it. This book provides an excellent starting point and is the basis for everything I present in these workshops.

Holding this book in your hands, dear readers, means that you have all of the basic principles at your fingertips. As always, the road to perfection is long and winding. My most heartfelt advice is simply this:

practice, practice, practice.

Best Sales Strategies That Gets Customers Excited

Joachim Guenster

11 Online Course

How to get Customers and Investors Excited to Throw Money Your Way!

Why do we remember “Little Red Riding Hood” after so many years? Does the name “Mr. Spock” ring a bell? On the other hand, why do our prospects forget our presentations 10 minutes after we leave their office?

Wouldn't it be great to have the answers to these questions? It certainly would be if you wanted to sell something. Oh, you're not in sales you say? Are you sure?

When was the last time you wanted to persuade your co-worker to follow your lead? Or the last time you wanted your spouse to go along with your ideas? Or the last time you wanted to convince your boss to give into the crazy idea of giving you a raise? Here's the simple truth: These are all sales opportunities. Plain and simple! You want to close the sale, don't you?

Well, now you can.

This course will teach you how to build bestselling stories and sell anything to anybody at anytime. No rocket science, just simple easy methods for everybody.

You will get step by step instructions.

You will get secrets elicited from the world's best: Steve Jobs, Stephen Spielberg, and many others.

You will see best practice cases. Real cases from my successful customers.

You can learn how to become a StorySculptor yourself and help others to craft bestselling stories.

It's Easy, Convenient and Simple to learn. And it has a lot to do with "Little Red Riding Hood," "Snow White," the legendary "Mr. Spock," and many other stories that we remember. Good stories stick, while our sales pitch almost never does. Good stories are remembered, while our sales pitch goes in one ear and out the other. Good stories sell! While our sales pitch doesn't (most of the time).

So how do we change our sales pitch to convince our prospects and turn them not only into happy customers, but into raving fans?

Well, in short, we need to tell a story!

That's it! A story will do it!

In this online course you will find the strategies you need to build an awesome story which excites, will be remembered, and which will be retold many times over.

Come on and join! You won't regret it!

FULL Udemy MONEY BACK GUARANTEE in effect!

GET YOUR SPECIAL DISCOUNT FOR THIS COURSE WITH THE BELOW LINK

www.udemy.com/storysculptor/?couponCode=US+Buch

Sorry, as this is a printed book, you will need to type the URL into your browser. If you access the site directly you may use this code „US+Buch" If something comes up which is not working please write me a quick e-mail and I´ll help you jg@storysculptor.net

12 Live Seminars

People are often taken aback upon reading this book and find their minds riddled with questions. Can you truly sell without the facts? Who is my villain? How can I develop a strong opening? What anchors should I use?

I get asked these questions constantly. First things first: don't expect overnight improvement. You need to live with these techniques and put them into practice, so be patient with yourself. I cannot over-emphasize the importance of practice.

What follows is a description of some of my most popular seminars. Check my blog for the latest dates and times and for the newest ticket information. Just visit my website here:

www.storysculptor.net

13 Thank you

Thank you for accompanying our hero on his journey. I hope that you had fun and learned a lot of useful information. Of course, there are many other techniques that can improve your storytelling even more, and I want to offer those to you, too. Please sign up with your email address to receive notifications on when our hero will have another adventure!

Sincerely yours,

Joachim Guenster

StorySculptor

Printed in Great Britain
by Amazon